SPEAKING YOUR MIND
WITHOUT STEPPING ON TOES

D1004673

SPEAKING
YOUR
MIND
WITHOUT
STEPPING
ON TOES

HENRY A. VIRKLER

Guidelines for Group Leaders Included

VICTOR BOOKS®

A DIVISION OF SCRIPTURE PRESS PUBLICATIONS INC.
USA CANADA ENGLAND

Library of Congress
Cataloging-in-Publication Data

Virkler, Henry A.
  Speaking your mind without stepping on toes / Henry A. Virkler.
    p.   cm.
  Includes bibliographical references.
  ISBN 0-89693-399-7
  1. Assertiveness (Psychology)—Religious aspects—Christianity.
  2. Christian life—1960—   I. Title.
  BV4647.A78V57   1991
  248.4—dc20   90-27752
                                               CIP

1 2 3 4 5 6 7 8 9 10 Printing/Year 95 94 93 92 91

CONTENTS

Preface

PART I

RESPONSE STYLES

1.	Five Ways to Relate	11
2.	What's Your Style?	27

PART II

RELATIONSHIP-ENHANCEMENT ASSERTIVENESS

3.	Developing Social Skills	43
4.	Deepening Friendships	63

PART III

SELF-PROTECTIVE ASSERTIVENESS

5.	What Does God Say About Self-Protective Assertiveness?	85
6.	Self-Awareness: A Prerequisite to Self-Protective Assertiveness	112
7.	The Triple-A Model of Assertiveness	130
8.	Responding to Detours	149
9.	The Art of Negotiation	166
10.	Reinforcing Your Message with Nonverbal Behavior	175

Afterword	193
Guidelines for Group Leaders	196
Notes	201

To
Stephen Berleth
and in
loving memory of
Helen Berleth

PREFACE

Assertiveness is the ability to express your thoughts, feelings, beliefs, and desires in direct, honest, appropriate ways that do not violate the rights, needs, and self-esteem of another person.

Assertiveness is a style of living, a healthy way of interacting. Not only does it help you deal with negative feelings that arise when someone's priorities conflict with yours, but assertiveness also helps you reach out to people and deepen your friendships.

Assertiveness involves communicating your needs in ways that show care, respect, and affirmation for the other person as well as for yourself. For Christians, both lay and clergy, assertiveness means learning to speak the truth in love.

But why a new book? Don't other books and articles teach assertiveness skills? Yes, they do, but many of these books have weaknesses. Some early secular assertiveness books suggested communication tactics that were manipulative and sometimes obnoxious. Some techniques were "counter-manipulative" (designed to counter a manipulative person) but so frustrating to the recipient that they could hardly be called *assertive* (since assertiveness involves speaking the truth *in love).* People who read those books and attended assertiveness classes based on them often alienated friends, spouses, or employers with their newfound "skills."

A second weakness of many secular assertiveness books from a Christian perspective is that they never attempt to reconcile assertiveness with biblical concepts such as turning the other cheek, humility, servanthood, and preferring another over oneself.

A few Christian assertiveness books do deal with the biblical perspective and encourage the reader to be assertive, but stop short of actually explaining the all-important "how-to."

This book will attempt to address some of these weaknesses. First, it will examine the teachings of contemporary assertiveness in light of teachings from God's Word. Second, it will help you learn to "speak the truth with love" through practical exercises that are relevant to your life. Third, it will help you be assertive without being aggressive by learning to build affirmation into assertiveness. Finally, it will help you learn how to remain assertive and positive, even when people attempt to detour you back into a nonassertive style.

This book will be more helpful if *experienced* rather than merely read. I suggest that you do two things to get the most benefit from it:

First, if you aren't already part of a study group, try to find two or more people who share your interest in becoming more assertive. Even if your group consists only of a few close friends who are committed to learning assertiveness, you can work your way through the chapters and exercises in this book together. The group interaction—helping you analyze, assess, and practice new ways of behaving—is an important part of learning assertiveness. The Guidelines for Group Leaders in the back of this book will help your group practice your new skills in a supportive, constructive, group setting.

Second, buy a notebook for answering questions and keeping a journal. You'll get much more from this book if you write your answers to the questions as you go through each chapter. Also, the exercises you work through individually often serve as the basis for discussions in group sessions.

Best wishes as you learn to speak the truth with love!

Henry A. Virkler, Ph.D.
Snellville, Georgia
1991

PART I
Response Styles

O N E

Five Ways to Relate

There is so much more to be gained from life by being free and able to stand up for oneself and from honoring the same right in others.

—Robert Alberti and Michael Emmons

Bob and Marie came for counseling in the twenty-fifth year of their marriage.[1] Charles, their older son, had just graduated with a business degree from a prestigious university, and Mark, the younger, was a sophomore music major at an equally well-known college.

Bob and Marie were well-liked and actively involved in the church where they were longtime members. They appeared to have a happy, stable marriage. Friends came to them for advice and counseling, and their attractive home was often the scene of parties and activities.

That warm picture of contentment was shattered within minutes of Bob and Marie's arrival for their first counseling session.

"I've just filed for divorce," Marie began cautiously.

Bob's voice wavered as he spoke. "We're going through this counseling sort of as a last resort. We really need help."

They were hurting too deeply to play games. Quickly, the difficult story poured out from two tortured lives.

"I've been unhappy in the marriage for as long as I can remember," Marie confessed. "But two years ago, when our younger son was finishing high school, I knew I would some-day ask Bob for a divorce. I've waited for Mark to be fully established in college. Now the time has come."

It was evident from the ensuing conversation that Bob had been caught completely off guard by Marie's decision.

"Sure," he said, "early in our marriage we had some rather angry disagreements, but those episodes gradually stopped. I mean, we haven't had a serious dispute in years."

"Looking back now," Bob continued, "I know there have been lots of times when I could tell from Marie's facial expressions or her silence that she was upset. But since she didn't *say* she was upset, I assumed that her annoyance was minor, that she would soon get over it. I had no idea things were this serious, until she told me about the divorce! I mean, I know I'm not a perfect husband, but . . . divorce? At first I thought she was kidding!"

Marie was hardly joking. In fact, the bitterness was so deep that she would not reconsider her decision, despite several counseling sessions that she begrudgingly attended. She refused to listen to pleas from her pastor, their devastated sons, and shocked friends.

"It's all over," Marie announced at their final counseling session. "Too much pain has been buried all these years."

They did divorce. To her friends, Marie seems bitter and withdrawn. Bob appears to be coping, but he is confused by what happened and he suffers bouts of depression. He has buried himself in his work as a business executive, a tactic that has proven only partially successful in dealing with the emotional aftermath of the divorce.

This painful divorce need not have happened. If Bob and Marie had been aware of the unhealthy patterns in their relationship, they could have taken measures to change their styles of communication. The problems that destroyed Bob and Marie's marriage and devastated their parents, their sons, and their friends *could* have been avoided.

We bring expectations into every relationship, whether parent/child, husband/wife, minister/church member, employer/employee, or friend/friend. Often, we never talk about those expectations; we just assume that the other person will realize what we want. Sometimes, in fact, we may not even be aware of our own expectations in a relationship until the other person fails to meet our unspoken, unconscious desires.

When someone doesn't meet our expectations, we begin to feel disappointed, hurt, or frustrated. At that point we have a choice. We can respond in one of five ways: passively, aggressively, passively-aggressively, manipulatively, or assertively.

Our response style can include both how we initiate action and how we respond when someone else initiates an action toward us. Let's look at each of the five response styles.

The Passive Response Style

> *A man who trims himself to suit everybody will soon whittle himself away.* —*Charles Schwab*

> *An appeaser is one who feeds a crocodile, hoping it will eat him last!* —*Winston Churchill*

Passivity manifests itself in a variety of ways. We respond passively when we fail to express our disappointment, hurt, or frustration. We say yes when we really want to say no, permitting others to speak for us, or allowing them to make decisions about our lives with which we disagree. A passive person may try to make a point (stand up for feelings, desires, or needs), but does it so timidly that others readily coerce or intimidate the passive person into doing things their way. Consider the following scenario:

Mother: "Julie, I'd like you to clean up your room. We'll be having company this evening and—"

Julie (interrupting): "My room is perfectly fine! It's just as picked up as any of my friends' rooms are!"

Mother (quietly and a little timidly): "Julie, you have dirty clothes lying on the floor and under your bed. Your bed isn't made and there's a wet towel—"

Julie: "Well, if you don't like my room the way I keep it, why don't *you* do something about it? You don't have anything to do while I'm in school anyway!" Julie abruptly goes to the family room, slamming the door as she leaves. She turns the stereo on at a deafening volume.

Mother resignedly straightens up Julie's room so that she won't be embarrassed when company comes.

Although her mother's initial statement sounds somewhat assertive, Julie knows from past experience that she can easily intimidate her mother back into passivity. Mother invites Julie to intimidate her:

- by talking softly and timidly.
- by allowing Julie to interrupt her and unilaterally termi-
nate the conversation without reprimanding her.
- by cleaning Julie's room for her.

The passive person usually rehearses "if only" dialogues
through his or her mind: "If only I had said . . . If only she
were more. . . ." Still, when the next similar conversation
occurs, the passive person often responds in the same old
pattern.

When we're passive, we sacrifice our own wishes, feelings,
and desires in order to be accepted by others. We inhibit
ourselves from expressing personal preferences. We feel and
act like victims, rather than taking responsibility for how we
will allow our relationships to develop. We apologize for having opinions and hold our true feelings inside. We act shy,
timid, and embarrassed. We try to avoid disturbing anyone.
We often lack confidence in our own judgment. In short, the
passive person says, "I count you; I don't count me."[2] We
maximize the importance of the other person's thoughts,
feelings, and goals but minimize the importance of our own.

Passive people sometimes feel okay about themselves, at
least temporarily, because they believe they're acting in a
Christian manner. They are turning the other cheek, returning good for evil. However, in the long run, passive people
often feel depressed because they don't reach their desired
objectives. They may be frustrated because other people
don't take their feelings into consideration when making decisions. They may feel tense, in part because they are afraid
their frustrations might erupt against their will and jeopardize
their relationships.

This happened in the case of Bob and Marie. For many
years Marie kept her everyday frustrations inside for fear
that if she expressed any of them, they would all come out in
one gigantic explosion. Eventually, however, her suppressed
anger turned into bitterness.

The passive stance is a *powerless* stance. Powerlessness
and lack of control over one's life usually lead to low feelings
of self-worth. If we are passive we should recognize that
others can't "put us in our place" all by themselves. *We*

choose to go there. If we don't accept the role another has found for us, we don't have to play it. As Eleanor Roosevelt aptly said, "No one can make you feel inferior without your consent." Julie's mother needs to realize that Julie doesn't have the power to intimidate her unless she in some sense cooperates with her.

The Aggressive Response Style

Julie's responses to her mother illustrate the aggressive response style. We respond aggressively whenever we try to reach our goals in ways that do not respect the needs, feelings, goals, or self-esteem of other persons around us. Julie was aggressive by:

- never investing the effort to understand why a clean room was important to her mother.
- interrupting her mother twice.
- leaving the conversation abruptly and unilaterally.
- blocking her mother out by playing the stereo.

All of these behaviors say, "I count me, I don't count you."[3]

Aggressive behavior can result from having a personal goal blocked by someone else's behavior. Julie's goal was to not have to clean her room. When her mother's request blocked that goal, Julie became angry and frustrated.

Likewise, when someone blocks one of our goals, we usually feel frustrated at that person. If we allow that anger to come out without modifying it in some way, it will usually manifest itself in aggressive behavior.

Goals that frequently are blocked by other people include:

- arriving someplace on time.
- completing a task without being interrupted.
- having a few minutes of peace and quiet with no demands from anyone.
- being able to eat supper without telephone interruptions.
- not being criticized.
- not being disagreed with.

All of us become aggressive at least occasionally. Usually the purpose of our aggression is either to punish the person who has blocked us from reaching a goal, or to intimidate that person into withdrawing the action that blocked us.

Aggressive responses may be either mild or severe. We may use aggression only occasionally, or we may use it regularly. Aggressive responses include name-calling, blaming others, talking at or down to people, and interrupting them. Aggressive responses also may include speaking for others, railroading them to agree with us, and insisting on having the last word. More intense forms of aggression include intimidation through haughtiness, snickering, glaring, or physical violence. Some teenagers and adults keep their families in a constant state of intimidation simply by suggesting that they might engage in physical violence if they are not allowed to have their own way.

Aggressive behavior usually prompts an initial feeling of satisfaction if the person achieves his or her desired goal. However, the long-term result of continued aggressiveness is usually low self-esteem. Aggressive people know that they are alienating family and friends, and they feel guilty and depressed about their behavior. Remorse about the destructive effects of their aggressiveness may be covered by a gruff and distant facade. Even when aggressive people are sorry for their behavior, their remorse may not be noticed because other people are too busy trying to stay out of their way. Aggressive people may continue their quarrelsome behavior because they feel lonely and misunderstood.

The Passive-Aggressive Response Style

A third response style includes characteristics of both the passive and aggressive styles. Passive aggression—indirect aggression—usually begins when people either allow someone to do things which bother them or when they fail to tell someone when he or she isn't doing what they expect of him or her. Eventually the irritations accumulate and begin to come out in indirectly aggressive responses.

Suppose Julie's mother had been passive-aggressive rather than passive. She might be frustrated by Julie's messy room, but rather than talk with Julie about this directly, she might express her frustration in any of the following ways:

● being less friendly toward Julie—without telling her why.

● failing to do some of the things she normally did for Julie—without saying why.

- being tardy about getting some of Julie's things done as a way of retaliating for Julie's messiness.
- discussing with other mothers how irresponsible Julie is.
- not allowing Julie to participate in some activity—without telling her why.,

Passive-aggressiveness may manifest itself through hostile humor, sarcasm and ridicule—the kind Archie Bunker often used against his wife and son-in-law. Sarcasm and ridicule may be employed either passive-aggressively or aggressively as a form of intimidation. The difference is that aggressive sarcasm used to intimidate usually occurs *during* the situation, whereas passive-aggressive sarcasm or ridicule may slip out several hours or days *after* the situation. The recipient of passive-aggressive sarcasm may have difficulty figuring out what caused the outburst.

A type of passive-aggressiveness that Christians frequently use is withdrawal of attention or affection. The good-night kiss becomes perfunctory or doesn't happen at all. The cheery "Hello, I'm home" doesn't happen or isn't responded to. Family members give each other "the silent treatment." In this case silence doesn't simply mean that no one is talking; the silence is intended to send a very powerful message—"I don't like something you've done and I'm withdrawing from you to show you how much I don't like it." Christians frequently use this type of passive-aggressiveness because it seems less unChristian than other types such as ridicule, sarcasm or hostile humor.

The passive-aggressive style can stem from a subconscious attitude that says, "I don't count me." The person doesn't identify his or her needs or feelings and doesn't ask others to consider his or her needs or feelings *at the time.* Then later, as anger festers, it erupts in behavior that says, "I don't count you." Thus, in the passive-aggressive style, the rights and feelings of neither the intitiator nor the recipient are respected.

If we continually respond in a passive-aggressive style, our self-concept is eventually lowered. As mentioned earlier, passive persons may occasionally feel good, because they see themselves as good Christians when they let others have their own way; and aggressive people may occasionally feel good about getting their own way. But passive-aggressive people rarely feel good about themselves. When we're being passive-aggressive, our initial passive responses make us feel powerless in social situations. As we brood over the wrongs inflicted on us, we become bitter. Delayed indirect responses offer little satisfaction and often alienate family and friends.

The Manipulative Response Style

A fourth way of responding to differences in expectations between people is by manipulation. Whereas aggressive people attempt to coerce someone to change by angry threats and intimidation, manipulative persons use more indirect and frequently psychological means to get their way.

For example, one mother would never tell her daughter openly and directly what she desired, but whenever the daughter would deviate very far from what she wanted, the mother would rush into her bedroom, fling herself onto the bed, and cry hysterically, "I don't know what I'm going to do with you," or "You're going to drive me crazy!" A father told his ten-year-old daughter that he would return to the family *if* she got straight A's in school. Another mother claimed to have heart pains whenever her family or friends broached a subject she didn't want to talk about. Aggressive people usually try to produce *fear of themselves* as a way of getting what they want. Manipulative people usually try to control others by producing a different kind of fear—the fear that if other people do not do what they want them to, something terrible will happen.

• Manipulation can take several forms. We can compare the other person with some hypothetical ideal: "Any Christian who really loves the Lord would/wouldn't . . . Any *good* husband would/wouldn't . . . Why can't you be like your brother (sister, kids at church)?" Children quickly learn to use the same manipulative strategy: "I wish you were like my friends' parents. *They* let them . . ."

• A second form of manipulation is guilt-inducing statements like: "After all I've done for you, how could you do this (or fail to do this) for me?" "If you really love me, you would . . ." "If you don't quit doing that, you'll drive me crazy (make me commit suicide, etc.)." "God won't love you if . . ."

● A third method of manipulation involves emphasizing details that place the other person in an unfavorable light. For example, a husband who wants his wife to change her behavior can rattle off a list of things she does inadequately, without noting any of the positive things she does. Such manipulation is often effective, especially if the wife feels so negative about herself that she thinks she must give in to his demands, since she is apparently performing inadequately in so many other areas.

● A fourth form of manipulation is whining—used skillfully by children and some adults. People will often give in to the whiner because they want to be free of the noise the whiner makes. Because it works, some people continue this method throughout life.

In all forms of manipulation the manipulator, like the aggressive person, operates from an "I count me, I don't count you" position.[4]

Even though they may feel satisfied momentarily when their manipulation achieves its desired goal, people who habitually use manipulation seldom feel good about themselves. They realize how destructive their methods are to relationships, and can't respect themselves because their methods, though successful, are unhealthy and unfair. In their more honest moments, they feel guilty for the hardship their self-centeredness causes others.

Unfortunately, manipulative people seldom admit any of the above problems. Like aggressive people, they usually cover over any feelings of sadness with brusqueness, irritability, and an air of self-righteousness.

The Assertive Response Style

Assertiveness includes two basic sets of skills: relationship-enhancement skills and self-protective skills.

Relationship-enhancement skills include the ability to initiate, maintain, and end conversations comfortably with strangers, friends, or family. They include the ability to give encouragement and compliments comfortably, and to receive compliments from others without discounting them. They also include the ability to express love and affection appropriately, and the ability to deepen relationships when desired.

Self-protective assertive skills include the ability to discuss our thoughts, feelings and wishes without undue anxiety, even among strangers or in hostile situations. Assertive people can disagree with others without apologizing. They can comfortably refuse requests from others which conflict with their own priorities. Assertive people can defend themselves against accusations which they consider to be unfair or inaccurate. They can express anger or annoyance in ways that respect the feelings and self-esteem of others. Similarly, they can deal with someone else's anger comfortably and nondefensively. Finally, they can make reasonable requests of others.

Let's replay our scenario between Julie and her mother, this time with Julie's mother taking a more assertive stance:

Mother: "Julie, I'd like you to clean up your room. We'll be having company this evening and—"

Julie: "My room is perfectly fine! It's just as picked up as any of my friends' rooms are!"

Mother (with gentle firmness): "Julie, you are not to interrupt me when I'm speaking to you. The issue is not what your friends' rooms look like. The issue is that your room is not acceptable *to me* in light of the fact that we will be having company this evening. You have dirty clothes lying on the floor and under your bed. Your bed isn't made, and the wet towel lying on it has made your sheets and blankets all wet. I want you to clean up your room and bathroom to my satisfaction before you do anything else this afternoon."

Julie (exasperatedly): "O Mom! Terri was coming over right after school and we were going to the mall. Why do you have to be so unreasonable?"

Mother (normal tone of voice): "I don't think it's unreasonable to expect you to clean up your room each day. You know you are to do this before leaving for school each morning. If you had done these things then, you wouldn't be needing to now.

"Also, you know that we have a family rule that you are to check with your father or me before making plans with your friends. I'm sorry if you and Terri are frustrated about not being able to go to the mall this afternoon, but you wouldn't be in this difficulty if you had observed our family rules."

Julie (pouting tone): "Why can't you just close the door to my room when the company is here?"

Mother: "I could, but that wouldn't change the fact that you have dirty clothes to put in the wash, a damp bed that needs changing, and at least forty-five minutes work to get your bedroom and bathroom looking presentable.

"It's not just for company's sake that we keep the house picked up. The family has to live here seven days a week. Your father and I have made a joint decision—we believe it's fair and reasonable to expect each family member to do a share of keeping the house attractive and picked up. You and your friends may not agree with our rule, but while you live with us you must abide by our rules.

"You may either try to call Terri now and reschedule your trip to the mall, or you may wait until she gets here and tell her of your change in plans then."

Julie (recognizing that her mother is not going to change her mind): "Okay."

Assertive people are usually respected because they are not passive, aggressive, passive-aggressive, or manipulative. They are not manipulatable or easily intimidated. Assertive people make choices about what they will do with their time, energy, or money, rather than being forced into situations by others. Assertive people are actors, not only reactors. Because they can say no, the assertive person's yes really means yes. Those who are usually successful at manipulating or intimidating others may dislike assertive people, but they will consciously or unconsciously respect them.

When we're assertive, we relate to others from an "I count you, I count me" frame of reference.[5] When we show consideration and respect for others, we do not feel guilty about how we have treated them. And when we count ourselves, we maintain our own self-respect. Because we make choices about how we are going to respond to others and to life, we see ourselves as actors rather than victims.

Assertiveness not only is rooted in a healthy self-esteem, but it also produces healthy self-esteem. As we feel good about ourselves, we are able to count ourselves and others.

As we count ourselves and others, we feel good about the way we are treating ourselves and others.

You may be assertive in some situations and relationships and nonassertive in others. For example, you may have good relationship-enhancement skills, but relatively weaker self-protective skills. Or, you may be assertive with young children but not with your spouse or employer. The exercises in this chapter and the next are designed to help you identify those areas where you would like to become more assertive; the remainder of the book should give you help in becoming more assertive in those areas.

KEY IDEAS FROM CHAPTER ONE

The five basic ways you can relate to others are:

1. The Passive Response Style—maximizing the importance of the other person's thoughts, feelings, and goals and minimizing the importance of your own. (The "I count you. I don't count me" attitude.)

2. The Aggressive Response Style—trying to reach your goals in ways that do *not* respect the needs, feelings, goals, or self-esteem of other persons around you. (The "I count me. I don't count you" attitude.)

3. The Passive-Aggressive Response Style—using indirect aggression. Passively allowing others to do something you do not want them to do or failing to tell others when they are not doing things that you would like them to do, then punishing them by silence or sarcasm. (The "I don't count me. I don't count you" attitude.)

4. The Manipulative Response Style—responding to differences in expectations between people by indirect, frequently psychological means, to get your own way. Using fear of something bad happening to manipulate others. (The "I count me. I don't count you" attitude.)

5. The Assertive Response Style—consisting of relationship-enhancement skills and self-protective skills. Relationship-enhancement skills include the ability to initiate, maintain, and end conversations comfortably, and the ability to give and receive compliments and encouragement. Relationship-enhancement skills also include the ability to express

love and affection appropriately and to deepen relationships when this is mutually desired.

Self-protective skills include the ability to discuss your thoughts, feelings, and wishes without undue anxiety, even among strangers or in hostile situations. They also include the ability to refuse requests that conflict with your priorities and defend yourself against inaccurate accusations.

EXERCISES

1. For the following two situations, write in your notebook the name of the response style each person is using and the reason why you think it is that particular response style.

A. The James family has decided to go out for dinner Friday evening, but the destination has not yet been determined. Each of the four children and two adults has different preferences and tastes, making the decision difficult. When asked where the family should eat, each responds as follows:

• Jim, fifteen, says his preference is McDonald's because it's nearby and has quick service. Jim needs to be back home as soon as possible so that he can get to a concert on time.

• Mom has a preference but doesn't offer it because she knows there will be enough conflict without adding any more options to the family's decision-making process.

• Jeff, thirteen, insists on going to an Italian restaurant but predicts, "Nobody will want to go there anyway, because you *never* do what I want to do!"

• Jennifer, sixteen, wants to go to a Greek restaurant, but won't speak up because she *knows* her Dad never does what the women in the family want to do. When they finally arrive at the chosen restaurant, she lets it "slip out" that she is resentful about being there.

• Mary, twelve, lets the family know that she wants to go to Kentucky Fried Chicken, then proceeds to explain (in no uncertain terms) why each of the other suggested possibilities is a "stupid" choice.

B. For their anniversary Jim and Janice go out for a candlelight dinner at a posh restaurant. The Friday night crowd keeps the couple's waitress "hopping." She seems pleasant and competent, but extremely busy. When Jim's "rare" steak arrives, it is well done.

Consider the following scenarios and identify each response style used and the reason you think it is that particular response style.

• Jim says nothing, eats the steak, and leaves a two-cent tip for the waitress.

• Jim says nothing, eats the steak, but obviously does not enjoy the meal. Still, he leaves a normal tip.

• Jim calls the waitress to the table, loudly denounces her for the steak she served, and demands a new one cooked to his previous specifications.

• Jim eats the steak and leaves a reasonable tip. But during the next few months, he caustically tells several friends about the lousy meal he had there.

• Jim gestures for the waitress to come to his table. He acknowledges how busy she is but explains that he received a well-done steak when he had ordered a rare one. He asks her to return it to the kitchen and have it replaced with one cooked as he originally requested.

2. Read each of the following situations, and then write five responses for each one. Compose a passive response, an aggressive response, a passive-aggressive response, a manipulative response, and an assertive response.

• Jane and Bill have been married for six weeks. Before the wedding, Bill seemed to respect Jane's opinion; however, since the honeymoon, Bill regularly discounts Jane's opinions and puts down her preferences. Jane senses the difference and could respond in any of five ways:

• Phil and Carolyn have been married twelve years. Carolyn kept her weight at an attractive level for the first decade of marriage, but during the past two years she's been adding extra pounds and inches. Phil is aware of several thoughts and emotions: (1) he feels angry at Carolyn's lack of self-discipline; (2) he feels concern for her health; (3) he knows she doesn't feel as good about herself now that she's overweight; (4) he's not as attracted to her as he used to be. How might Phil respond to Carolyn?

● Jan is a freshman at a state university. This is the first time she's been away from her hometown for any extended period. Her roommate and most of the girls in the dorm are actively dating. Jan has been asked on a few dates, but she hasn't accepted any because she believes, from what her friends have said, that most of the guys expect more than a good-night kiss.

Jan would like to date, but she doesn't want to compromise her strong convictions regarding sexual involvement before marriage. She has decided to accept a date the next time she is asked by someone desirable, even though she knows she may be faced with an uncomfortable situation. How might Jan respond if her date initiates some activity she deems unacceptable?

3. Before you learn how to be more assertive, you need to identify your current response styles. One of the best and most accurate ways to identify the styles you use is to keep a personal journal for the next four or five days. In your notebook write the following headings: Situation and date; My behavior; How I felt; My response; What I should have done; Why I didn't do what I wanted.

Although a journal requires some effort, the few moments of time you spend each day will help you see patterns in your own behavior and identify the reasons you choose particular responses. Start a journal today and continue it for one week.

MY ASSERTIVENESS JOURNAL

Situation and date	My behavior	How I felt	My response	What I should have done	Why I didn't do what I wanted
Monday evening. Friend called during supper and talked for ten minutes.	Made gestures to wife about how long the person was talking.	Irritated at caller. Tense that wife would be angry.	Passive	Explained to friend that we were eating supper and asked if I could call him back in thirty minutes.	Afraid he would consider me impolite.
Tuesday morning. Reviewing notes for class at 10 A.M. Student asked to see me for "just a minute."	Listened, but was increasingly cold as conversation dragged on.	Frustrated, especially as I realized student had done this before.	Passive-aggressive	Clarified with student whether it was a one-minute conversation. Made an appointment if it was to take longer.	Did not want to seem unfriendly. Wanted to be seen as easily approachable by students.
Wednesday morning. Had to attend a reception.	Developed excuses about why I couldn't go.	Anxious	Passive	Viewed the reception as an opportunity to see old friends and make new ones.	Told myself that I would probably do something wrong socially.

TWO
What's Your Style?

If I can't say no, I can't really say yes. Because if I can't say no, others will never know if my yes really means yes, or if it only means I'm afraid to say no. Thus others will only know that my yes is a genuine yes if they know that I can say no when I want to do so.

—Author Unknown

After reading chapter 1 and completing the exercises, you should be able to identify and describe five different ways people can respond when they are disappointed, angry, or frustrated in a given situation. You may use more than one style, depending on the situation and the person with whom you are dealing. It's not uncommon for each of us to be assertive in some areas, and nonassertive in others.

Chapter 2 has three major purposes. By the time you have completed this chapter, you should be able to identify

● the styles you use in various situations.

● what you say to yourself, consciously or subconsciously, as you choose a particular style.

● three kinds of situations in which you would like to become more assertive.

This chapter is as much a "doing" chapter as it is a "reading" chapter. The exercises at the end are extremely important. Also, keep up with your journal throughout this week to help you identify the styles you use in various situations.

In chapter 1 we examined five different response styles— passive, aggressive, passive-aggressive, manipulative, and assertive. These response styles affect not only how we choose to initiate interaction with others, but also how we respond to others when they initiate actions toward us.

The main ideas in this chapter are based on four assumptions we make about these styles. Let's look at them.

Assumption One

Our response style usually can be understood in terms of one or more of the following:

Our parents' response styles.

The role we played in our family of origin.

The experiences we have had with emotionally significant people since leaving our family of origin.

• After examining his responses for a week, Bill recognized that when his wife did something that displeased him, either by doing something he didn't want her to do, or by not doing something he wanted her to do, he would withdraw from her and be quiet. After thinking about this, he realized that he had seen his father do the same thing. Bill remembered seeing his father's father react similarly. Thus, the same passive-aggressive pattern had been perpetuated for three generations by each male modeling his father's example.

• Patricia has strong convictions about Christian wives being submissive, and she tries to live out those convictions. She rarely speaks up about things that annoy her, and seldom gets angry. However, in keeping her journal she saw that she occasionally makes a very critical or caustic remark which seems to "come out of nowhere," or is out of proportion to the incident that triggered it. She is dissatisfied with herself for making these sarcastic comments. What do you think is happening here psychologically, and what response style is this?

As Patricia thought about this, she realized that her mother had strong convictions about submission and that she also struggled with making occasional sarcastic comments. Patricia remembered how uncomfortable she felt about her mother's sarcasm, and how she had promised herself that she would try never to say such things to her husband. Patricia continues to repeat patterns she saw in her parents, even though she has strong feelings against the behaviors.

• Faye spends most of her time helping others. People say she has the gift of mercy. She rarely does things for herself, and she always puts other people's needs ahead of her own. Much of the time this is a very fulfilling role for Faye to play: she enjoys the respect that other people show her and the good feelings she gets from knowing she has ministered to others. However, sometimes she gets tired of always being the one who does the giving. When she occasionally asks people to listen to her needs, they are so accustomed to her being the comforter that after they've listened to her for a few moments, they turn the attention back onto themselves.

Faye is experiencing a great deal of personal stress right now, and she is becoming increasingly resentful that no one seems to care about her problems. In thinking about this in terms of the models her parents provided, she sees little resemblance between her constant care-giving and the behavior of either of her parents. Her father left the family when she was two, and was never heard from again. Her mother tried to work and care for the children, but her caring was sporadic and at times nonexistent.

Faye was the oldest of the three children. In examining her role in the family, she realized that she coped with her anxiety about being abandoned by becoming a substitute mother for her younger brother and sister. She received a great deal of affirmation from her mother, both sets of grandparents, and other adults for being so mature and thoughtful. The substitute mother role became one she assumed more and more frequently. Faye realizes now that the role she constantly plays with her friends in adulthood is a continuation of the one she played in her family as she was growing up.

• Carol was raised by a healthy, loving Christian couple. Both parents show a strong respect for themselves and each other, and are healthily assertive. Carol married a congenial young man a year after their high school graduation. The first few years of marriage seemed normal, with the typical challenges of early marriage. Now, ten years later, Carol seems to have lost much of her earlier joy and spontaneity. They visit her parents together only occasionally, and Carol usually comes alone.

Carol rarely attends church anymore, and they seldom visit with other people, even though they once had many close friends. Carol has dropped out of many recreational activities she used to enjoy. She has become shy and reserved, and there is often a look of pain and sadness on her face during unguarded moments.

What has happened to Carol? Few people know that her husband has a drinking problem. Every night on the way home from work, he picks up two six-packs and begins drinking nearly as soon as he gets in the door. Carol has withdrawn from her parents because she's embarrassed to let them know how drunk he gets each evening. She has withdrawn from church and social relationships for the same reason. In fact, she has discontinued her involvement in all outside activities because her husband resents her when she goes out in the evening or spends money.

As a result of the drinking, their marriage relationship has deteriorated. Carol finds it impossible to discuss anything with her husband, including his drinking. She has become less and less assertive because she fears that he might become physically abusive. Her husband, who is often irritable and negative, gives her no affirmation, and she has withdrawn from the family and friends who could give her support and positive feedback.

As a result, Carol's self-esteem has taken a nosedive, and she has less of the self-confidence necessary to be assertive or to do things independent of her husband. Carol came to realize that her response style is a result of the experiences she has had with an emotionally significant person since leaving her family of origin.

Assumption Two

We often continue to use a given interpersonal style out of habit, even though our present relationships may be very different than the ones where we originally developed our response style. Our style is not usually the result of a conscious choice or careful examination, but is a habit that's been continued over the years.

As we grow up in our family of origin, we often find that a particular style seems to work best or is safest to use. Sometimes children find that the only, or the most effective way to get their needs met is to be aggressive, passive-aggressive, or manipulative. When we leave our family of origin we often continue to use that same style out of habit, even though that particular style may not be the healthiest or most appropriate one to use in our new environment.

For example, many women grow up assuming they are to be passive, helpless, and dependent. When some of these women enter professions, they find that if they don't change these unconscious assumptions and behavior patterns, their professional careers will be hampered.

Children of alcoholic parents develop patterns of passivity and compulsive obedience to rules because they find that this is the safest way to live with an alcoholic. When the children become adults, they often carry these assumptions into relationships where these conclusions are no longer necessary.

Assumption Three

We frequently use a given interpersonal style because we have convinced ourselves (by the subconscious things we say to ourselves) that a particular style is best for our situation.

The majority of people who use a passive style do so because they believe this style is safer, more Christian, or more appropriate than other styles. Likewise, people who use an aggressive or manipulative style do so because they believe, either consciously or subconsciously, that it is the most effective way to get what they want. People who use a passive-aggressive style often start out trying to be passive; but then the repressed anger comes out later, sometimes against their will, frequently because they cannot contain their anger any longer.

Dennis, a shy business major, was afraid to take the initiative with women his age because of the things he said to himself, sometimes consciously, sometimes subconsciously. Some of these self-statements included:

– "If I tried to talk to a woman, I'd probably say something stupid and really embarrass myself."

– "If someone got interested in me I wouldn't know how to handle it, and that would really be awful."

– "If someone got close to me they'd see what I'm really like, and they'd reject me."

Sometimes people are convinced that assertiveness is best in most situations, but they remain nonassertive in one or more specific areas of their lives. For example, Phabrice was healthily assertive with her husband, children, and friends. However, with one of her bosses, she had withdrawn. Whenever possible, she found reasons not to attend the staff meeting he usually chaired. For several months she was not even aware that she was avoiding his meetings.

In thinking about this, Phabrice realized that in the last few staff meetings she had attended, she had shared some strong concerns of hers. Each time this boss had listened to what she said but then had not followed up on these matters. She felt hurt and angry that he didn't seem to take her point of view more seriously. She had subconsciously begun to say to herself that there was no point in being assertive with him or even in attending his staff meetings. He wouldn't act on her concerns when she expressed them anyway.

One of the best ways to change the way we feel is to change our way of thinking. In his rational-emotive therapy, Albert Ellis has created and popularized the ABC Theory of Emotion.[1] As the diagram indicates, A stands for the activating event, B for the belief we bring to that event, and C for the emotional consequence we have as a result.

A	+	B	$\longrightarrow$	C
Activating		Belief		Emotional
Event				Consequence

The activating event is what happens; the belief is what we say to ourselves either consciously or subconsciously about the meaning of A, and the emotional consequence is the feelings we have as a result of our beliefs.

Let's use the example of Dennis to understand how the ABC Theory of Emotion works. In this instance the activating event was the possibility of interacting with a woman his own age. Dennis' beliefs included several examples of what has been called "disabling self-talk." Dennis emotionally disabled himself when he told himself the following:

– "If I tried to talk to a woman, I'd probably say something stupid and really embarrass myself."

– "If someone got interested in me I wouldn't know how to handle it, and that would really be awful."

– "If someone got close to me they'd see what I'm really like, and they'd reject me."

Therefore, Dennis' beliefs produced anxiety, the emotional

consequence. Similarly, Phabrice produced a sense of futility about attending staff meetings, by saying to herself that her boss didn't take her opinions seriously anyway.

If we are going to change the feelings that keep us from being assertive, we must change the conscious and subconscious self-talk that produces feelings of anxiety or futility about the worthwhileness of being assertive.

Assumption Four

We are more likely to change our behavior and to use new skills if we are convinced that the new skills represent a better way of relating.[2] At a practical level, how can we convince ourselves that it is wiser, healthier, or better to be assertive than to use one of the other response styles? Ellis' rational-emotive model provides a helpful answer here as well. The full model is diagrammed below:[3]

$$A \quad + \quad B \longrightarrow C$$

A		B		C
Activating Event	+	Belief	→	Emotional Consequence

or

A		D		E
Activating Event	+	Dispute	→	New Emotional Consequence

As an alternative to moving from the activating event to a belief then to an emotional consequence, we can choose to dispute with our initial anxiety-producing thoughts and move from the activating event to **D** and then to a healthier emotional consequence or **E**. (**B** stands for thoughts that produce dysfunctional feelings; **D** stands for thoughts that produce healthier, more appropriate emotions.)

We dispute with our beliefs by consciously evaluating their validity and changing our self-talk. For example, Phabrice was feeling a sense of futility about the value of going to staff meetings, because she believed that her boss didn't take her opinions seriously. After thinking about the situation, she was able to come up with several **D**s (disputing thoughts).

Some of these were:

– Her boss has asked her opinion on several things in the last six months.

– Her boss has sometimes failed to follow up on suggestions or complaints made by others in staff meetings as well.

– Perhaps her boss didn't follow up on her ideas because he had other things on his mind during the staff meeting, not because he didn't take her ideas seriously.

Phabrice realized that it was not healthy professionally for her to avoid future staff meetings. She started to say things to herself such as:

– "It's important to attend staff meetings."

– "I have good ideas to share."

– "It isn't essential for the boss to affirm every idea or complaint that I make."

– "If I offer an important idea and no one picks up on it, I can always state how important I think that idea is, and ask the group to discuss it at the next appropriate time."

As a result of this self-talk, Phabrice began to feel better about staff meetings and soon started attending them and contributing again.

Similarly, Dennis talked with his counselor about some of the self-talk he was doing. His counselor helped him examine his fear that he might say something embarrassing or stupid. They discussed how Dennis felt toward others who occasionally said things incorrectly. Dennis began to realize that even his pastor whom he respected very highly said things imperfectly, sometimes even in a sermon in front of several hundred people! Dennis realized that when his pastor could laugh at his own mistakes, he helped everyone realize that it was Okay to be imperfect. He saw that if people know that you genuinely care about them, they don't demand that you be perfect. By saying these things to himself, Dennis found he could reduce his fear that he must converse perfectly in order to be accepted.

Dennis' counselor also got him to reevaluate his self-talk about not being able to handle someone getting interested in him. Dennis soon recognized that healthy friendships usually develop gradually and that this development gives both people time to think about the next step they want to take. He realized that if he became anxious about how to deepen a friendship, he had several resources he could look to—books on the subject, his counselor, Christian friends he respected, and very importantly, his own thoughts and creativity. Thus he soon had several healthy disputes he could use against the disabling self-talk he had been saying to himself.

KEY IDEAS FROM CHAPTER TWO

1. Our response style usually can be understood in terms of one or more of the following: Our parents' response styles, the role we played in our family of origin, or the experiences we have had with emotionally significant people since leaving our family of origin.

2. We often continue to use a given interpersonal style out of habit, even though our present relationships may be very different than the ones where we originally developed our response style. Our style is not usually the result of a conscious choice or careful examination, but a habit that has been continued over the years.

3. We generally continue to use a given interpersonal style because we have convinced ourselves that that particular style is best for our situation.

4. We are more likely to change interpersonal styles if we consciously evaluate and change our subconscious assumptions. We are more likely to change our behavior if we are convinced that a change will produce a healthier style.

EXERCISES

This chapter and the exercises that follow have three major purposes:

– To help you identify the styles you use in different situations with different people.

– To help you determine what you say to yourself (either consciously or subconsciously) as you choose a particular style.

– To help you identify three kinds of situations in which you would like to become more assertive.

The following exercises are extremely important if you are

to receive maximum benefit from this chapter. They will help you look at your present levels of assertiveness, understand how you became the person you are, and help you identify your personal goals for improving the quality of your life. Write your answers to the following questions.

1. A helpful step in understanding your own response style involves looking at your parents. Your parents often served as important role models, and no doubt they still influence how you deal with frustration and anxiety-filled situations.

Use the following questions to help you describe how each of your parents dealt with specific situations. Write your answers in your notebook so that you will have as much space as you need to elaborate on your answer. If you knew only one parent or if you were raised by someone other than your parents, alter your answers accordingly, but base your responses on the person(s) who filled the most significant parenting role during your childhood.

For all the questions under number 1, give three answers:
–Father?
–Mother?
–Which one are you most like?

● Relationship-enhancement skills
    a. How comfortably could your parents initiate, maintain, and end conversations as desired?
    b. How comfortably could your parents give compliments?
    c. How comfortably could your parents receive compliments without discounting them?
    d. How comfortable were your parents in expressing love and affection to others?
    e. How well were your parents able to deepen friendships when they desired to do so?

● Self-protective skills
    a. How comfortably could your parents state their own feelings, beliefs, wishes, attitudes, or rights?
    b. How comfortably could your parents disagree with someone else's point of view?
    c. How comfortably could your parents refuse requests

which conflicted with their own priorities?

d. How well could your parents defend themselves against unfair or inaccurate accusations?

e. If your parents were frustrated or irritated, which one of the five response styles did they usually use?

f. How did your parents usually deal with someone else's anger?

g. How comfortably could your parents make reasonable requests of others?

h. Overall, which of the five response styles most accurately describes each of your parents?

2. Keep an assertiveness journal this week (last exercise in chapter 1). After completing it, review the journal in preparation for doing the Personal Assertiveness Inventory.

3. Complete the Personal Assertiveness Inventory[4] on the next page using Y for yes, N for No, and S for sometimes.

4. Go back through the Personal Assertiveness Inventory and circle the three areas where you marked No or Sometimes which you would most like to change. Specify the area and the category of persons involved. Write down those three areas in your notebook. For example:

a. I would like to be able to maintain conversations comfortably with my in-laws.

b. I would like a deeper friendship with my spouse.

c. I would like to be able to refuse my children's demands when they conflict with my own priorities.

5. Try to identify the conscious and subconscious self-talk that keeps you in a nonassertive response style in these three areas.

PERSONAL ASSERTIVENESS INVENTORY

Relationship-enhancement Skills	Friends of the same sex	Friends of the opposite sex	Spouse, boyfriend/ girlfriend	Parents and in-laws	Children	Authority figures, Bosses, etc.	Business contacts, salespeople	Strangers
Can initiate conversations as desired								
Can maintain conversations								
Can end conversations as desired								
Can give compliments								
Can receive compliments without discounting them								
Can express love and affection comfortably								
Can deepen relationships when desired								

Self-protective Skills							
Can state my own feelings, beliefs, wishes attitudes or rights							
Can disagree with someone else's point of view comfortably							
Can comfortably refuse requests which conflict with my priorities							
Can defend self against unfair or inaccurate accusations							
Can express anger and annoyance assertively							
Can deal with someone else's anger comfortably and non-defensively							
Can make reasonable requests of others							

PART II
Relationship-Enhancement Assertiveness

THREE

Developing Social Skills

Live a life of love, just as Christ loved us.

—Ephesians 5:2

When we think of assertiveness, we often think first of self-protective skills. However, self-protective assertive skills are only half the story. An assertive person is also able to initiate and maintain comfortable relationships with people through relationship-enhancement skills such as:

- The art of encouragement,
- The ability to receive compliments,
- The ability to converse comfortably,
- The ability to express love and affection, and
- The ability to deepen friendships.

God's Word and Relationship-Enhancement Skills

An assertive Christian needs all these relationship-enhancement skills to maintain the closeness and fellowship that Jesus intends for His followers:

> As the Father has loved Me, so have I loved you. Now remain in My love. If you obey My commands, you will remain in My love, just as I have obeyed My Father's commands and remain in His love. I have told you this so that My joy may be in you and that your joy may be complete. My command is this: Love each other as I have loved you (John 15:9-12).

The love described in these verses has many aspects: God's love for us and our love for God; our acceptance of our own worth and lovableness; and our love for other people. Most Christians would agree that God wants us to have interpersonal habits and skills that allow us to love others deeply and be loved by them in the same manner. Christians also recognize that the basis of that love is God's love for us—a basis that secular assertiveness does not recognize.

The writers of Scripture always portrayed people in terms of their relationships—to God and to other people. As part of the body of Christ, none of us can say, "I don't need you" (see 1 Corinthians 12:12-26; Romans 12:3-5). We long for relationships because God created that desire within us. Genesis 2:18 says, "The Lord God said, 'It is not good for the man to be alone, I will make a helper suitable for him.' " Our need for companionship exceeds the husband-wife relationship. We function best when we also have healthy, mutually supportive relationships with friends, parents, children, co-workers, brothers and sisters.

Emotional isolationism is not an option for the Christian committed to obedient scriptural living. Love and hospitality to friends and strangers are strongly emphasized throughout the Bible. The following is but a sample of the verses that exhort us to reach out to others in kindness and love:

● "Love your neighbor as yourself" (Leviticus 19:18b).

● "Do to others as you would have them do to you" (Luke 6:31). Notice how much more is encompassed here than if Jesus had said: "Don't do unto others what you wouldn't want them to do to you." Jesus commands us to take the initiative in building relationships and doing good deeds.

● "Be devoted to one another in brotherly love" (Romans 12:10a).

● "Share with God's people who are in need. Practice hospitality" (Romans 12:13).

● "Carry each other's burdens, and in this way you will fulfill the law of Christ" (Galatians 6:2).

● Keep on loving each other as brothers. Do not forget to entertain strangers, for by so doing some have entertained angels without knowing it" (Hebrews 13:1-2).

● "Love one another deeply, from the heart" (1 Peter 1:22b).

● "Above all, love each other deeply, because love covers over a multitude of sins. Offer hospitality to one another without grumbling. Each one should use whatever gift he has received to serve others, faithfully administering God's grace in its various forms" (1 Peter 4:8-10).

● "Make every effort to add to ... godliness, brotherly kindness; and to brotherly kindness, love. For if you possess these qualities in increasing measure, they will keep you from being ineffective and unproductive in your knowledge of our Lord Jesus Christ" (2 Peter 1:5, 7-8).

● "We know, and to some extent realize, the love of God for us because Christ expressed it in laying down His life for us. We must in turn express our love by laying down our lives for those who are our brothers. But as for the well-to-do man who sees his brother in want but shuts his eyes—and his heart—how could anyone believe that the love of God lives in him? My children, let us love not merely in theory or in words—let us love in sincerity and in practice!" (1 John 3:16-18, PH)

Biblical love is not simply the *absence* of doing wrong to others, and it's not piously talking about love at a theoretical level. Biblical love involves reaching out to a brother or sister in need of companionship, encouragement, physical or financial help, and helping that person in any way we can.

However, it is one thing to know that we should be hospitable, warm, and loving, but it's quite another to know how to do this comfortably. No one is born with the ability to initiate, maintain, and deepen relationships. These are learned skills, and many of us, particularly males, reach Christian adulthood without learning these skills. Some of us grew up in situations where the emphasis was on competitive sports, academics, or working long hours rather than on developing relationships. In other homes, close relationships were discouraged or risky, or were labeled effeminate.

Here are some beliefs that may keep us from taking the time and risk to develop close relationships.

– I don't have the time to spend on a deep friendship.

– Whenever I've tried to develop a relationship, something has always gone wrong.

– It's safer not to let anyone get too close.

– I was really taken advantage of in the last relationship I developed, and I'm not going to let that happen again.

– I don't know how to get started, so I'd probably make a fool of myself if I tried.

Most people who reach adulthood without developing relationship skills spend their lives assuming they can never change. But the good news is that we aren't locked into our past behavior and beliefs. We can challenge our assumptions and we can develop the skills that will enable us to experience the richness that only deep friendships can bring.

In this chapter we'll look at three assertive social skills that apply to any relationship, whether it be with a casual acquaintance or a best friend or spouse. In the next chapter we'll look at those relationship-enhancement skills that are particularly applicable to special friendships.

Giving Encouragement
Bonnie and Bob Brown were not satisfied with their daughter's habit of calling them only once a month. Recently Brenda's calls were even less frequent. In many ways, Bonnie and Bob had no reason to worry about her. At twenty-four, Brenda was an active member in her church and her job as a chemical engineer produced a good income for her.

"If only Brenda knew how much we missed her and were concerned about her!" Bob complained. "I just wish she'd let us hear from her more often—a minute on the phone or even a postcard. We call her often, but we always get her answering machine, and she doesn't like us to call her at work."

"We've tried every way we know to get her to call us more often," said Bonnie. "Everything we do just seems to make things worse." "Everything" included criticism for her infrequent calls. As a result, Brenda called even less often.

As part of an assertiveness-awareness exercise in conjunction with a church study group, the Browns began writing down what they said to Brenda during her telephone calls. The pattern was a shock to both of them.

"Just about every other sentence," Bob confessed, "was something critical of her. I never realized..." his voice trailed off.

"We were trying to get her to call us more," admitted Bonnie, "but what we were doing had the opposite effect. Frankly, I don't blame her—considering what we said."

Once they saw the damaging effect of their criticism (a passive-aggressive response style), they began thanking

Brenda when she called. No pressure, only encouragement. Soon her longer calls returned to a once-a-month frequency. The Browns noticed a difference in Brenda's attitude toward them. Sometimes she telephoned every week or so "for just a moment" to let them know about an especially rewarding day at work.

• Motivate through encouragement. People are more likely to act the way we want them to if we reward and encourage. We all have defense mechanisms that react against criticism and haranguing. The saying, "More flies are caught with honey than with vinegar," holds true.[1]

Research has shown that people who encourage others are more likely to be perceived as sympathetic, understanding, and attractive than those who don't.[2] We must look for and speak of the positive in others, if we would want them to look for the positive in us.

Encouragement produces an environment in which people feel secure and able to grow. G.H. Mead described a concept he called "reflected appraisals."[3] According to Mead, part of our self-concept comes from appraisals that other people reflect back to us. Normally, when people give us positive feedback, we feel good about ourselves. Negative reflected appraisals (or no appraisals) make us feel less secure, less loved, and less worthwhile. When we are around people who criticize, we begin to feel insecure, unaccepted, and inadequate. Few people can grow in such an atmosphere. If we desire to nurture personal growth in others and if we want them to enjoy being around us, we must encourage much and criticize little.

If we want a person's behavior to be affected, we must learn to encourage even small positive changes and ignore negative actions. If we focus on encouraging positive behavior, the negative behavior often will stop without any explicit negative feedback.

Encouragement is one of the most vital elements in any healthy, long-term human relationship. Marriages, for example, often begin to turn stale when the "romance"—feelings generated in part by acts of kindness and encouragement—is replaced by "expected" duties. When a loved one stops thanking us for our positive actions, we feel as if we're being taken for granted, and the joy begins to go out of the relationship.

• Learn to see the positive. While giving encouragement and compliments is neither difficult nor costly, it's something we often fail to do. Why is that? We fail to praise others because we often don't see anything to praise. We focus so strongly on the negative qualities that we convince ourselves the person can't possibly deserve our praise. Let's explore how we arrive at those perceptions.

You are bombarded with countless pieces of sensory data every moment of every day. Though you may not be consciously aware of it, at this moment your brain may be registering the sensations of a chair pressing against your back and legs. Even if the room is relatively quiet, your ears are picking up numerous sounds. Your hair is resting against your scalp. Your wristwatch band is pressing against your wrist. Your belt is encircling your waist. But you don't focus on each of these stimuli all of the time.

Because you can't possibly attend to countless stimuli at the same time, you use a process called *selective attention* or *selective awareness*. Your brain sorts through the stimuli and focuses attention on the most important ones. That pattern of sorting sensory stimuli, tuning in to some and ignoring others, goes on without any conscious awareness that you are selectively attending to some things and not to others.

In this same manner, people who tend to be positive and encouraging have developed the habit of looking for positive things in people and affirming those things. Those who are critical have developed the habit of focusing on what is wrong with people and remarking about these things.

What do you notice, for example, when you first enter a room? Do you initially see what is out of place, smudged, or mismatched? Or do you glance around and focus on what is in place and pleasing to your eye? When your child comes down for breakfast, do you spot and comment on what's disheveled and incorrect, or do you first see and affirm what's right?

Many of us first react to the negative. Our reaction is based on two subconscious assumptions:

– The best way to change people is to tell them what they're doing wrong.

– If we don't say anything negative, people will know we're satisfied with them.

Probably both of these assumptions are incorrect. It is not true that if we don't say something negative, people will know we feel positive toward them. Particularly if most of what we *do* say is negative, they are likely to believe that the absence of feedback from us also means we're displeased with them, but just not displeased enough to tell them so. This is true for adults as well as for children. *The best way to let people know that we're satisfied with them is to tell them so.*

The assumption that the best way to get people to grow is to tell them what's wrong with them is also probably wrong. Occasionally we need to give negative feedback because it's dangerous to allow people to continue to do certain things or because it's sometimes inefficient to give the person constructive guidance in any other way. However, if most of our feedback to others is criticism, people are likely to feel so anxious or angry in our presence that they make more mistakes because of the anxiety we cause them; they may not be able to learn new ways of doing things because the anxiety we cause them interferes with their learning of a new skill; or the negative feelings caused by our constant criticism destroy or reduce their motivation to want to please us.

● Give positive feedback. People grow best in an atmosphere where they feel accepted and loved; they learn new skills best when they feel relaxed and not pressured to be perfect. Most of us *want* to please other people when we feel accepted and respected by them. If the main form of feedback we give is encouragement, we can occasionally offer constructive criticism without it causing undue anxiety or hurt.

Learning to be an encourager involves becoming aware that we may be selectively focusing on what is wrong with people, and making a conscious effort to begin looking for things to affirm. The longer our criticism has been going on, the more detrimental an impact we may have made, and the harder it may be to find areas to affirm. However, we can learn to find something positive to affirm in almost anyone. Here are four possible areas which can be affirmed:

Behavior (father to son): "Mark, I appreciate the way you helped pack the car for our picnic today."

Effort (mother to three-year-old daughter): "Donna, thank you for sitting quietly through most of the church service. I know you tried very hard, and I appreciate what you did" (with no mention of the times Donna squirmed).

Appearance (wife to husband): "John, I'm really proud of how you've stuck to your exercises. You're looking great!"

Possessions: "Jim, that's a beautiful van! It will be great for family vacations."

Let's summarize our discussion on relationship-building to this point in the following statements:

1. God's Word repeatedly reminds us to love one another.

2. One of the best ways to show love to those around us is to be an encourager.

3. One of the best ways to produce an environment where people feel secure and able to grow is to look for things to affirm in them.

4. If we have developed the habit of looking for what's wrong in others, it may take a conscious effort on our part to begin to focus on the positive. We may need to remind ourselves consciously to look for positives on a daily basis until this new habit becomes established in our minds.

5. If most of the feedback we have given to family members or employees is negative, the most effective way to ensure that they know that we're satisfied with them is to explicitly compliment them.

Virginia Satir, an internationally known family therapist, claimed that we all need about eight hugs a day to feel healthy.[4] It isn't always possible to give eight physical hugs a day, but we can "hug" people through our words of encouragement.

Receiving Compliments

As you start to encourage and praise others, you'll probably receive more compliments yourself. At present, when you receive a compliment, how do you respond?

- Do you turn away and mumble something to yourself?
- Do you deny the validity of the compliment?
- Do you discount the compliment?

• Do you change the subject without acknowledging the compliment?

People who deny or discount compliments generally have either a low self-esteem or falsely assume that those who accept compliments will become conceited.

People with low self-esteem often reject compliments and positive reflected appraisals because the feedback is incompatible with their view of themselves. By doing this, they continue to hold on to their negative self-concept. The positive appraisals necessary for them to change their negative self-concept do no good because they refuse to let them in.

Compliments do not necessarily lead to conceit. To be conceited involves believing that you are better than others, or failing to recognize where your abilities come from. Compliments can help you develop a healthy awareness of the strengths God has given you. Accepting compliments can lead to greater freedom in using your strengths for God and for others.

When someone says something nice to you, do them and yourself a favor: accept the gift. A simple "Thank you" is sufficient. Or "It makes me feel good to hear you say that." Forget the discounting explanations! Then consciously let the compliment become part of your emerging self-concept.

How does accepting compliments allow you to move closer to others? First, people feel more comfortable with you if you can accept their positive reflected appraisals. You know people who are always doing things for others, but will never allow anyone to do anything for them! You would feel closer to them if they allowed you to repay their kindnesses once in awhile. Similarly, people will feel closer to you if you allow affirmation to flow freely in both directions.

Another important way in which receiving compliments allows you to move closer to others is this: When you receive compliments from others, you become more comfortable with who you are, and when you are more comfortable with who you are, you can allow others to get closer to you. If you feel inadequate, you are less likely to let others get close, for fear that they will see what you're really like.[5] Therefore, being willing to receive compliments increases your self-esteem and you become more comfortable with close relationships.

Becoming an Interesting Conversationalist

Conversation is the framework on which a friendship is built. Most of us can make conversation in certain contexts, but we find it more difficult in others.

Dudley, for example, is comfortable with one or two people, but going to a large gathering, such as a company party or class reunion, makes him extremely nervous.

Jim is the life of any party or social gathering. At church he leads the congregational singing and the men's prayer breakfast. But at home he has trouble carrying on a conversation with his wife or teenagers. He usually spends most of his time watching television or working on the yard.

The bad news is that people who are unable to carry on comfortable conversations often feel lonely and inferior in large social groups and may have very limited relationships even with those who would like to be their friends. The good news is that we can change more easily than we think! To become a good conversationalist we need to develop skills in six basic areas: Conversation openers, self-disclosure, listening, picking up on "free information," conversation closers, and breaking in. Let's look at these.

● Conversation openers. You can begin a conversation with *three topics:* the *situation* you're in, *the person* you're addressing, or *yourself.* The situation, especially one that may interest or puzzle both of you, is usually a safe and good conversation opener. Asking about the other person is another good option, as long as your questions are not too personal and as long as the other person is open to talking. Talking about yourself is usually the least preferred option, for as Dale Carnegie wrote: "You can make more friends in two months by becoming interested in other people than you can in two years by trying to get other people interested in you."[6]

We can begin conversations with *three methods:* by asking a *question,* by voicing an *opinion,* or by stating a *fact.* Often the best conversation openers combine two of these. For example:

– "Hello. My name is Jim. Do you mind if I sit here?" (stating a fact and asking a question)

– "I really enjoyed that service. What did you think of it?" (voicing an opinion and asking a question)

– "I couldn't help but notice how well prepared you were for your presentation to the board of directors. Where did you get those statistics for your cost analysis?" (voicing an opinion and asking a question)

Questions asked alone or in combination with statements of fact or opinion can be effective in promoting further conversation. Questions can be categorized as either close-ended (those that can be answered with a yes or no or with a specific piece of information) or open-ended (those that require a more comprehensive answer). For example:

– "Do you mind if I join you?" is close-ended.
– "How long have you been attending this class?" is close-ended.
– "How did you choose accounting as a career?" is open-ended.
– "What kinds of new projects are you working on?" is open-ended.

Obviously, open-ended questions are better conversation openers since they foster further discussion. Because close-ended questions ask for only factual information, they need to be followed immediately by other questions in order to keep the conversation going. Here are some suggestions for using questions as effective conversation openers or discussion starters:

Use specific rather than general questions. Specific questions are easier to answer than general ones. For example, the questions "Tell me about yourself" or "What do you believe?" are so broad that they often make it difficult for the person to know how to begin. It's better to phrase a question more specifically, such as "How do you like college?" or "What do you think about . . . ?" (a specific topic or situation)

Start with general issues rather than personal ones. General issues are less intrusive and threatening than personal ones. Move gradually to more personal issues only when it's clear that both of you are comfortable with this.

Initial conversations usually proceed along the following progression: You first give *facts* (name, vocation, where you live), then *opinions* (perceptions on certain issues), and finally *feelings* (personal emotions and beliefs relating to life issues). In some initial conversations you may only get to an exchanging of facts. Occasionally if an initial conversation is extended and is going well, there may be an exchanging of opinions on selected issues. Usually the sharing of feelings happens during later conversations.

Ask questions that allow people to respond in either direction on controversial issues. If you ask leading questions (questions that imply the way you expect the other person to respond), you are likely to cause the other person to want to end the discussion, particularly if they disagree with the direction in which you try to lead them. For example:

– "I think Christian rock music is of the devil and shouldn't be allowed in church. What do you think?" is a leading question.

– "Do you think Christian rock music has a legitimate place in church youth services?" is a better way of addressing the same issue.

To have good conversation openers available may require that we spend a little time before a social occasion thinking about who will be there and identifying some questions that would be good openers. Some good general conversation openers that can be used in many situations include:

– "Have you always lived in this area?" If they haven't, you can ask them to tell you about the areas they have lived in.

– "What kind of work do you do?" Follow this up by asking questions about the person's particular kind of work. If you are talking with a student, inquire about his or her field of study.

– "What do you think of . . . ?" (a current political or religious situation)

– "Would you tell me about your family?" Leave the question open-ended enough for single people to talk about their parents or siblings and for married people to talk about their spouses or children. Be aware that this question can lead into sensitive areas of childless marriages or divorces or separations. Ask follow-up questions only if you sense the person wants to talk further.

A little forethought can often provide you with excellent questions for the particular person you desire to talk to. Try to ask questions about which both you and the other person may share an interest. If you can find one or more such topics, you greatly improve your chances for an interesting conversation and a possible friendship. If you can't think of topics about which you're both interested, talk about things the other person cares about. You may learn some fascinating things.

• Self-disclosure. From beginning to end, a good conversation should include fairly equal amounts of self-disclosure from each person. If Peter talks too much about himself without allowing Paul an equal opportunity, Peter may seem egotistical, particularly if that imbalance lasts very long. Likewise, if Mary only asks questions about Jane without sharing much about herself, Jane may begin to feel as if she's being interrogated. A balanced sharing allows the conversation to be a true dialogue.

Good conversationalists will focus the conversation back on the other person after they have talked for a few moments themselves. They may do this by pausing when they notice the other person has something to say, or by asking a question that invites the other person to interact with what they have just said.

Problems may arise when you are talking with someone who is not a skilled conversationalist and does not know how to ask returning questions. In this situation you may have to initiate some self-disclosure, even if unasked. For example, if you've asked what kind of work the other person does, volunteer something about your own work. As discussed in the section on conversation openers, a conversation usually proceeds from facts to opinions and then to feelings. You should base the depth of your conversation and self-disclosure on what both you and your conversation partner seem comfortable with. Personal opinions and feelings may not surface in an initial conversation, especially if other people are around.

• Listening. A third conversational skill is listening. Keep in mind Dale Carnegie's advice about making more friends by becoming interested in other people than by expecting them to become interested in you.

One of the most important ways to show other people that you are interested in them is by showing an interest in what they have to say. Almost everyone has something to teach us about life, about how human beings function, or about themselves. But many people are convinced that they have nothing interesting to share. They will remain quiet unless you let them know that you are interested in hearing their story or their thoughts.

You can show interest in both verbal and nonverbal ways. Verbal ways include asking questions that show that you have been listening and would like to know more. Verbal ways also include suspending your need to express your opinion on every subject, and to disagree if the other person says something you don't agree with. This prayer from an unknown source humorously makes this point for all of us:

Lord, keep me from becoming talkative and possessed with the idea that I must express myself on every subject.

Release me from the craving to straighten out everyone's affairs.

Teach me the glorious lesson that occasionally I may be wrong.

Make me helpful but not bossy.

With my vast store of wisdom and experience, it does seem a pity not to use it all—but You know, Lord, that I want a few friends at the end! Amen.

You also can express interest—or lack of it—in nonverbal ways. A young boy tried to talk to his father, who was working at his desk. As the father continued shuffling papers, looking for something he had misplaced, the boy insisted, "Daddy, listen to me."

"I am listening," the father replied, as he continued looking for what he had lost.

The young boy tried to tell the rest of his story, but he was obviously disappointed by his father's inattentiveness. Finally he blurted out, "Daddy, please listen to me *with your face!*"

This story points out an important nonverbal way of showing people that you are interested in them—putting aside other things and giving them full eye contact. When you fail to give people the full attention of your eyes, they get the impression that you're more interested in something else. If you want to show someone else that you're interested in them, purposely give them undivided attention.

Two other ways of showing others that you're interested in them are not interrupting them when they're speaking and cultivating warmth in your voice. When you interrupt others, it's almost as if you're saying, "What I have to tell is more important than what you have to say." An important way of showing respect to others is to wait until they've completed their message before beginning yours.

Cultivating a "warm" voice is more subtle than not interrupting, but nevertheless important. Take a moment to listen to the sound of your voice as you carry on normal conversation. Is it harsh, unemotional, anxious, flat? If you find that it doesn't have the warmth that you would like, purposely focus on trying to develop a warmer conversational voice and see what happens.

● Picking up on "free information." Eventually most conversations will start to lose some of their energy unless this fourth conversational skill is used. Picking up on free information is a vital link to continuing a conversation.

When one or both persons involved in a conversation run out of things to say on a given topic, they have three alternatives. They can move on to another topic, stand there amidst an increasingly embarrassing silence, or end the conversation. Anyone who has done the latter two—and who hasn't?—would probably like to know *how* to go on to a new topic.

The best way to move ahead is by remembering information already given you. In almost any statement, there is some "free information" that can be used to move the conversation to a new topic once discussion of the present topic is finished.

For example, Susan asks Henry, "When did you move to North Carolina?"

Henry replies, "Ten years ago. Before that I lived in San Francisco."

For a while they continue talking about North Carolina, but Susan might eventually come back to the "free information" Henry provided and ask, "By the way, what was life like in San Francisco?" or "Why did you decide to move to the East

Coast?" Or Susan might decide to mention an interesting fact about San Francisco.

As you read the following conversation, pick out three pieces of "free information" Pastor Cortez could use to keep the conversation going. He's standing in a line to buy tickets for a high school football game when he meets a well-dressed young couple.

"Hello," he says. "I'm Juan Cortez, pastor of the First Church. We haven't met, have we?"

"No," the man replies, reaching out to shake the pastor's hand. "I don't believe we have. I'm Jim Perry, and this is my wife, Carla."

"I haven't seen you at any games before," the pastor continues, taking a step forward. "Are you from around here?"

"No," the young man says. "We just moved here from Pennsylvania. I wanted to see what the high school football games were like around here."

"Are you a football fan too?" Pastor Cortez smiles at Carla.

"Football's okay," she smiles back, "but I prefer some of the winter sports we had back home."

Can you identify at least three pieces of free information Pastor Cortez could use to help him keep the conversation going? As you go through the week, listen for free information in the conversations you carry on with others, and use that free information to move the conversation to a new topic after you've completed discussing the initial issue.

• Conversation closers. An assertive person should develop the skill of ending the conversation when he or she so desires. For instance, the trio in the previous illustration might have kept talking until the pastor reached the ticket booth. It would have been unwise to continue the conversation and hold up the rest of the line. But if Pastor Cortez were to merely turn around, buy his ticket, and walk off, he would risk communicating rejection or disinterest.

Effective closure to conversations affirms the other person and keeps the relationship open so that it can be resumed later. Pastor Cortez could have used any one of the following closings:

– "I really enjoyed talking with you."

– "I would enjoy having you visit the church where I pastor some Sunday. Good-bye now."

– "I hope you enjoy the game."

– "It's been nice talking with you. I hope you like living here."

• Breaking in. In addition to the five basic conversational skills, an assertive person should know how to comfortably enter a group conversation already in progress.

Whenever a number of people congregate informally in one room, the crowd breaks into several small groups. Some people seem naturally adept at mingling, moving from one group to another as they choose, while other people feel extremely uncomfortable in this kind of situation. This inability to move comfortably into already established groups is one of the things that makes some people uneasy with large social gatherings.

Breaking in is a skill that can be learned even by shy people. There are two basic steps involved in successfully entering an already established group. First, with your head and body held confidently, enter the group and *briefly* say or nod hello to each person there. This allows you to enter the group *physically* without significantly disrupting the conversation.

Secondly, listen until you understand the flow of the conversation and can enter the discussion without changing the pace that has already been set. This allows you to enter the group *psychologically.*

Remember that it's important for you to move into the group physically and psychologically. Don't passively stand on the periphery, hoping to be invited in. If you diplomatically move in physically, you are much more likely to have the self-confidence to become part of the group psychologically after you understand what the topic of conversation is.

If you are shy, you may feel uncomfortable with the two suggestions that were made in the previous paragraphs. Use the ABC Model from chapter 1 to identify beliefs that make you anxious about trying these two steps. You may find yourself using self-talk like:

– "If I tried to do that I might be ignored, and that would be awful."

— "If I tried to do that I might say something stupid, and I'd be embarrassed."

— "If I tried to do that I might not know what they were talking about, and that would be dreadful."

Try to identify the beliefs you are saying to yourself, and then see what disputing statements you can come up with.

Anyone can become a good conversationalist. All it takes is a willingness to practice the six skills we've discussed. In at least one conversation each day, try to use these skills and note what results you have. As with any new skill, you may feel a little awkward at first. But the more you use them, the more comfortable you'll feel with them.

KEY IDEAS FROM CHAPTER THREE

An assertive Christian needs relationship-enhancement skills to maintain the closeness and fellowship that Jesus intends for His followers. The skills include the art of giving encouragement, the grace to receive compliments graciously, the skill to converse comfortably, the openness to express love and affection, and the ability to deepen friendships. This chapter focused on the first three of these. The following chapter will focus on the process of deepening friendships.

EXERCISES

You may wish to spend two weeks working on these exercises before proceeding further in this book. Use the first week to work on the Criticism and Encouragement exercises, and the next week to work on the Accepting Compliments and Conversational Skills exercises.

Criticism and Encouragement

Criticism

1. Record in your journal both the encouraging and criticizing statements you made today and yesterday. Try especially to recall the critical statements that you made.

2. Count and compare the number of encouraging statements and the number of critical statements. Generally

speaking, if your ratio of criticism to encouragement is higher than one to four, that is, if you have more than one criticism for every four encouragements, people are apt to feel somewhat tense and anxious around you.

3. If you found that you encourage others less than you had hoped, identify possible conscious or subconscious reasons for your lack of encouragement. What might you be saying to yourself consciously or subconsciously that causes you to encourage less than you might want to?

4. Some people believe that giving out encouragement too generously will cause others to become conceited or cause praise to lose its effectiveness. Do you agree or disagree? Why or why not?

5. What are the differences between flattery and encouragement?

6. Look up the following verses and put each into everyday language, giving particular attention to words that speak of encouragement or edification (building someone up spiritually).

- Romans 15:5-7
- 2 Corinthians 10:8
- 2 Corinthians 13:10
- Ephesians 4:15-16
- Colossians 3:19, 21
- 1 Thessalonians 5:11
- 1 Thessalonians 5:14-15

Encouragement

1. Write out two encouraging statements to say to each of three people with whom you are in close contact.

2. Set some practical goals. If you have neglected encouragement, determine to offer a minimum of one encouraging comment per day to each person with whom you interact extensively; do this for one week. The second week, raise that goal to two compliments or encouragements per day. Remember, your ultimate goal should be to give *at least* four encouragements for every criticism. In fact, you will probably discover that as you become more encouraging, the "need" for criticism will drop considerably.

3. Write out at least two indirect encouragements (a posi-

tive statement made to someone who will probably pass it on to the person about whom you made the positive statement).

Accepting Compliments

1. For a few days keep a mental record of how you respond to positive comments that are made to you.

2. If you find you have difficulty accepting compliments, try to identify what self-talk is making it difficult for you to receive them. See if you can develop some disputing statements that will help you dispute the beliefs that are causing you the discomfort.

3. Identify a phrase (for example, "Thank you" or "Thanks") that you can use to accept a compliment graciously. When you receive a compliment, use that phrase to accept it. Then allow the compliment to soak in and become part of your self-concept. Identify any struggles you have with allowing this to happen.

Conversational Skills

1. Identify one or more areas or persons with whom you have difficulty starting or maintaining a conversation. Develop some conversation openers or topics for discussion that you could use in those situations.

2. Reread the section on becoming an interesting conversationalist and practice using the six conversational skills in at least one conversation each day. Identify which of the skills are easiest and hardest for you to use.

FOUR

Deepening Friendships

If a man does not make new acquaintances as he passes through life, he will soon find himself left alone. A man should keep his friendships in constant repair.

—Ben Jonson

The lesson of Charles Dickens' *A Christmas Carol* rings as clear today as it did in the days of the fictional Scrooge. We can be rich in money, but we are not truly rich if we have no friends. Only as we give our lives to others and develop deep friendships do we become truly wealthy.

What is a friend? Men and women frequently define what it means for someone to be a friend in somewhat different ways. For most women, a friend is someone with whom they have spent considerable time developing a relationship, someone with whom they've had a good deal of mutual sharing. For many men, a friend is someone with whom they've played a few games of golf or tennis; frequently they've had little or no deep, honest sharing.

Webster defines a friend as "a person one knows well and likes . . . an ally." A more complete definition of an intimate friend might be "someone whom you see on a regular basis, who knows you deeply and whom you know deeply." A friend is someone with whom you feel mutually comfortable sharing your most difficult temptations and struggles. Using that definition, how many intimate friends do most of us have?

If we're honest with ourselves, most of us hunger for at least one intimate friend. This isn't a sign of weakness, for God made us that way. In the Creation narrative the only time God said, "It is not good," was when He acknowledged that Adam had no suitable human companion. Even though Adam had a perfect relationship with God at that time, God recognized the importance of Adam's need for a close *human* friend. A theme repeated throughout the Old and New Testaments is that we need each other: we are not complete when we live in isolation (see 1 Corinthians 12:7-27; Romans 12:3-5).

Friendship and an Assertive Lifestyle
Genuine, intimate, healthy friendships develop best from an assertive lifestyle. Let's explore why the other four styles do not form a good basis for deep friendships.

• Passive people approach life from an "I count you, I don't count me" position. As a result their self-esteem is generally low, and they may not take the initiative in social activities that provide opportunities for friendship building. They frequently will not be aware of or use the conversational skills discussed in the last chapter. Passive people may genuinely care about others, but because they are often shy, others will not know this.

Some passive people are very good listeners and develop friendships with those who need someone to listen to them. These relationships are good in some ways, for they meet certain needs: talkative people want to be listened to and passive people want to feel worthwhile and "connected" to someone else. However, these friendships aren't as healthy as they could be because they're lopsided: one person does most of the sharing and the other person has few opportunities to share interests or concerns. Passive people may come to resent this, for it seems that others want to tell their problems but are too disinterested to listen in return.

• An aggressive lifestyle also is not a good lifestyle from which to build friendships. Don and Glenda came for marriage counseling because Glenda had separated from Don. Both wanted their marriage to be saved, if possible. As their story unfolded, Don related that he never saw his parents have a disagreement. Thus, he never saw a model of how two adults can discuss differences and negotiate a mutually-acceptable compromise. His father, a military career officer, ruled his family in an authoritarian manner; his word was law and there was no discussion about anything.

Glenda came from a family where her father was very aggressive and authoritarian toward her passive mother. She saw the pain this caused her mother for many years, and vowed to herself that she would never let this happen to herself in marriage.

When Don wanted something from Glenda he asked for it in the only way he had ever seen demonstrated in his own family—he demanded it. Glenda responded to his demands by remembering her promise never to allow herself to be treated in the same way that her mother had been treated. When Glenda refused to respond to Don's demands, he responded by louder and more belligerent demands. The verbal fights escalated, and then became physical as well as verbal.

Glenda's response to Don is not atypical. Most people withdraw from aggressive people unless they are too intimidated to even withdraw. By the time of the separation, Don's response to Glenda was almost entirely aggressive. When we discussed this, he realized what a negative impact his aggressiveness was having on the relationship. He thought his aggression was justified because of Glenda's separation from him. Unless Don is willing to cease using aggressive methods to try to get his way, he will lose his marriage.

People are wary of forming friendships with aggressive people. Even if aggressive people are usually friendly and have only occasional aggressive outbursts, people will be hesitant to get too close to them. In the following chapters we'll look at ways to deal nonaggressively with the frustrations that occur in every close friendship.

• Passive-aggressive responses are also detrimental to forming friendships. From the moment Sharon walked into the counseling office, her bitterness was evident. It came out in her words, her tone of voice, even in her tears. She was convinced that she had been mistreated by her first husband, her second husband, and now by her children. Her anger was so constant that it seemed to keep her from seeing reality as it actually was. For example, while close friends regularly spoke of how considerate and well-mannered her children were, all Sharon could see was the ways they were abusing her and taking her for granted.

People who are passive-aggressive may sometimes elicit our compassion because of the suffering and loneliness they inevitably bring upon themselves. But their loneliness continues, because most people will not choose to become close to a passive-aggressive person like Sharon.

Passive-aggressive people are not always as blatantly and constantly bitter as Sharon. Sometimes the passive-aggressiveness comes out sporadically, interspersed with periods in which the person is not overtly passive-aggressive. People are uncomfortable developing close relationships with the sporadic passive-aggressive, even during their periods of nonpassive-aggressiveness, for at least two reasons. First, having a friendship with a sporadic passive-aggressive is a little like walking through a jungle inhabited by a hostile enemy: you never know when you'll get caught in some unexpected sniper fire or step on a landmine. Second, when people criticize their friends behind their backs to us (even sporadically), we fear they may criticize us behind our backs to their other friends.

● Manipulative people also do not make good friends. They often get what they want in a relationship, attention and affection, but there is always a price tag. People resent being manipulated because the manipulator, like the aggressive person, is saying, "I count my needs, I don't count yours." Some skillful manipulators may be able to maneuver a situation without others even detecting that they are being manipulated. However, if manipulation is used regularly, others will sense it, even though they may not be able to detect how it's being done. As a result, they will keep their distance from the manipulator.

Mrs. Thurston is a manipulator. After her children grew up, they married and moved to various parts of the state. She missed them, and her loneliness intensified after her husband died in his early sixties.

Mrs. Thurston tried to get more attention from her children in a variety of ways, including telling them how lonely she was and what poor health she was in, listing all that needed fixing around the house, and complaining to each child about how the others were ignoring her. These were unconscious manipulative attempts to get them to visit her more often. The difference between this and passive-aggressive complaining is that in passive-aggressiveness the primary feeling is usually anger or bitterness. In Mrs. Thurston's manipulative complaining, the primary feeling was self-pity. The net result was that her children initially spent some time with her because her complaining made them feel guilty. However, they eventually resented her complaining and manipulation of them and began to withdraw—a common response to manipulative behavior.

• The best possible foundation for friendship is assertiveness. Assertive people enter friendships from an "I count my needs, I count your needs" position. As a result, they set up the expectation that relationships will involve give and take: sometimes mutual sharing, sometimes one person sharing and the other listening, and other times reversing those roles. This is a relationship where both people feel free to ask each other for what they need and to set limits on what they can provide. Both feel free to share their ideas, even when they may not agree. Theirs is a relationship where the biblical proverb is lived out: "As iron sharpens iron, so one man sharpens another" (Proverbs 27:17).

Counting the other person includes being trustworthy, being able to keep confidences, and being faithful to each other in our moments of weakness or failure. George Eliot captured the spirit of true friendship in these words:

> Oh, the comfort, the inexpressible comfort of feeling safe with a person; having neither to weigh thoughts nor measure words, but to pour them all out, just as they are, chaff and grain together, knowing that a faithful hand will take and sift them, keep what is worth keeping, and then, with a breath of kindness, blow the rest away.

Overcoming Obstacles to Developing Deep Friendships

Most of us have many priorities that compete for our time: our jobs, our families, our homes, and our church. Taking time to develop a deep friendship may not seem as important to us as these other activities. In a sense, developing friendships may seem self-centered because we are doing something for ourselves. But developing significant relationships is important to our mental and spiritual well-being. Probably none of us can be truly healthy for long if we do not have at least one deep friendship. Let's examine ways to overcome the obstacles to friendship.

• Making the time. When you think of developing friendships, you may say, "I don't have the time. My schedule is too full as it is." However, if you examine your schedule carefully, you may find time that could be used to develop friendships. For example, the average American adult spends ten to twelve hours a week watching television. You could take one evening per week to build friendships that would probably be at least as relaxing and probably more fulfilling than spending the same amount of time watching television.

Another possible way to build a friendship is to spend one lunchtime per week meeting with someone whom you'd like to know better. If this person works with you or nearby, meeting together may not necessitate making major changes in your schedule. Analyze your weekly schedule to see what opportunities you have to build friendships. One aspect of assertiveness is identifying what you want to do with your life, then organizing your time so that you accomplish the goals you have set for yourself.

• Focusing efforts on a few. We can get so busy making casual acquaintances that we have little or no time left to develop a few *deep* friendships. For the first year or two after Jim finished his doctorate, he was surrounded by many friendly people. Jim and his wife Sharon regularly invited people over for a meal or an evening, but didn't focus on developing more in-depth relationships with anyone in particular. Eventually they recognized that they were hungry for at least one set of friends with whom they had a special relationship.

From among their casual friends they selected one couple whom they particularly liked. Jim and Sharon began meeting with them every few weeks and developed a balanced friendship. Since none of the four had families living nearby, Jim and Sharon eventually asked the other couple if they'd like to become their "family." That was the beginning of a very special friendship that has continued for many years.

You can't possibly develop that quality of relationship with many people because of time constraints. Therefore it's important to select from your circle of casual acquaintances one or two or three people with whom you sense the potential for a deeper relationship. Concentrate your time with these people and then see if both of you desire to deepen the relationship.

● Overcoming fear. In the last chapter we discussed some of the debilitating self-talk that keeps us from initiating conversations in social situations. The same kind of self-talk can keep us from taking the risks involved in deepening relationships. For example:

– "If I invite her to lunch, she might say no, and I couldn't stand being rejected."

– "What if she says yes, and we don't have a good time?"

– "What if she tells everybody that I'm lousy company?"

For years Danny Thomas did a routine about a guy whose car ran out of fuel. During the walk to a nearby farmer's house, he explored all the disastrous possibilities. By the time he arrived to ask for a gallon of gas, he exploded with anger at the farmer because his self-talk had led him to the worst possible conclusion—that the farmer wouldn't give him any fuel.

Research by social scientists has shown that most of the things we fear never happen. Negative self-talk does nothing but build our anxiety, decrease our self-esteem, and keep us from venturing into friendships.

Most of us live as if our self-worth and acceptability depend on what other people think of us (reflected appraisals). When we do this, reaching out to develop friendships may cause us great anxiety because the other person may turn down our offer. If our self-concept is based primarily on reflected appraisals, then our self-confidence will not be very stable, for each day and each venture into a relationship could be the occasion for a rejection. If we want to have a stable self-concept that can provide the basis for taking risks in reaching out to people, we need to base our self-concept on something more solid than whether or not people are responding to us positively at this moment.

Does the Christian have a biblical basis for a secure self-esteem? The answer is yes! Every person who has accepted Jesus Christ can truthfully say the following things:

I am gloriously created by God, made in His image, and designed for fellowship with Him. I am deeply fallen; sin has entered into every part of my personality. Yet even though I continue to make mistakes and sin occasionally, I am wonderfully redeemed and fully loved. Even though God knows all about my fallenness, He redeemed me and fully loves me.

Therefore, I can accept myself because God accepts me. I can love myself because God says I'm lovable. I can feel okay, not because someone else says that I am, but because God says I am.[1]

If our self-acceptance is based on God's acceptance, then human refusals will not jeopardize our self-worth. If our self-acceptance is rooted in God's acceptance of us, then we need not be first in someone else's life in order to be okay. We need not be devastated if their priorities do not involve spending time with us or doing things with us, for our self-esteem does not hinge on their response to us.

Let's suppose that Dennis asks Linda to play tennis with him next Saturday, but she says no. Dennis could allow himself to be demoralized and decide not to take any more risks with women. He could say things like:

– "I guess I'll never make it with women."

– "I imagine she had someone more interesting to do something with on Saturday."

By basing his self-acceptance on who he is in the Lord, Dennis could be involved in more positive self-talk, such as:

– "Perhaps she doesn't like tennis or is busy next Saturday. I need to check out those possible explanations for why she turned down my invitation. Turning me down for one activity on one particular Saturday doesn't mean she doesn't want to do anything with me at any time."

– "Perhaps she's going steady with someone else, and I just don't know it. Or maybe she just isn't interested in dating anyone right now. If I make a couple more offers and she turns them down as well, perhaps she'll tell me what her reasons are. Either way, if she doesn't want to date, that doesn't mean I'm an unacceptable person. It may reflect her own attitudes and feelings about the place of men in her life."

– "It hurts to hear a no, but that doesn't necessarily mean she rejects me as a person. I'll never meet the person who might make a good friend or life partner unless I'm willing to take an occasional risk. I'm not going to let my fear keep me from taking risks."

● Taking off our masks. It's one thing to risk initiating activities with other people, but it's another to continue risking yourself to deepen a relationship. At some point, you need to decide just how much of your life you are willing to share with others and if you want to take off part or all of the social mask that most people never see behind.

We wear masks because we fear people would reject us if they *really* knew us, or because we fear they would not treat our vulnerability with the respect and tender care we want. If applied to casual relationships, both of these assumptions are partially true. It's not wise to share our deepest needs, feelings, or vulnerabilities indiscriminately.

However, if a relationship has been deepening gradually over time and if you sense this is a trustworthy person who would keep your confidence and genuinely care for you, you probably need not fear loss of confidentiality or receiving unsolicited advice. However, you still may be haunted by the fear that other people might reject you if they really knew you. Would they wonder, "If he's been a Christian this long, how can he still be struggling with *that?*" Or, "If she's really committed to the Lord, would she have those doubts?"

A committed friend will not judge you for your weaknesses. In fact, in a committed friendship, people usually draw closer as a result of honest communication. Think back to a time when someone risked rejection to share with you. How did you react when you saw how much trust that person had placed in you? You probably felt yourself drawn closer to that person. The same will usually happen for you. When you drop your mask, people will be drawn to you because of your willingness to be open. In a committed friendship, the more vulnerable you are willing to be, the closer you and your friend are likely to feel to each other.

No matter how much you theoretically agree with this, you are likely to feel anxious at the thought of actually revealing a vulnerable situation to a friend. In the last three months Hal has taken the risk to share deeply three times, once with his wife, and once each with two close friends. Each time he wrestled with most of the anxiety-producing thoughts identified above. Yet in each case the response was positive.

In the situation with his wife, Hal has found her to be increasingly sensitive in the area he revealed, and they have a stronger relationship as a result. One of Hal's friends responded empathetically to his need. He shared a deep struggle in his own Christian life, and they committed to pray for one another regularly as a result. In the third situation, Hal's friend confessed that he had the same struggle. They both experienced a strengthening of their own spiritual lives by sharing that struggle with each other (see James 5:16).

In the above examples, Hal experienced a significant deepening in his relationship with friends because of his willingness to be open; his friends indicated that the same happened for them. An almost euphoric feeling results when two people are willing to take off their masks and be fully real with each other, even if it be for only a few moments and in one area of life. Our relationships probably deepen in direct proportion to our willingness to be open and vulnerable. Unless we're willing to take the risk to let down our masks occasionally in the context of friendship, we probably will never experience the most exciting dimension that friendship has to offer.

● Allowing time and space. Intimacy must develop gradually. Pushing too fast often overwhelms one or both parties, causing at least one person to back away. Unfortunately, the more starved a person is for friendship, the more likely he is to want to get too close too fast. Just as with happiness, pursuing intimacy too rapidly often leads to disappointment. Intimacy is a by-product of doing things together and of sharing deeply *over an extended period of time.*

People not only need time to develop close relationships, but they also need space. Some human needs seem paradoxical: we desire closeness with another human being, but at the same time we desire distance, the ability to have some time and space to call our own. Some Gestalt psychologists have called this the need for contact and withdrawal. A healthy relationship allows both of these needs to be met; an unhealthy relationship often does not. As a result, one or both people may feel trapped or suffocated by the other person's dependency needs.

An example of this is Tim and Jackie's marriage. To outsiders, Tim seems to be a friendly, healthy person, but in reality he is very dependent on Jackie. When they get home from work, Tim resents any activity that takes Jackie away from him in the evening. He will pout or throw a temper tantrum until she gives up the activity, whether it be a women's Bible study, evening exercise, or a personal growth group. When he's watching television or a movie on their VCR, he does not even like her to be *reading* in the same room. He wants her sharing in the activity that he's doing.

As a result, Jackie feels like a prisoner in her marriage. She loves Tim and yet feels emotionally trapped. She would enjoy spending time with Tim, but when he *demands* that she spend every moment of her free time with him, she loses her ability to enjoy the marriage.

Friendship, whether it be in or outside of marriage, is something that we must allow the other person to enter by choice. When Tim doesn't allow Jackie some withdrawal time, the time she spends with him is a result of coercion rather than choice. Probably the only way that Tim and Jackie's marriage will improve will be for Jackie to be assertive about her need for some personal time, and for Tim to recognize that space is a valid and healthy part of any relationship.

● Realizing that friendships will change. There may have been a time when people could expect close friendships to last for a lifetime, with little change. People who expect such continuity in friendship today will probably become depressed and even resentful when a highly mobile and changing society causes them to be separated from their close friends.

Friendships may change for any number of reasons. Sometimes people move or are transferred. Sometimes job demands increase, leaving less time for friendship. Sometimes the birth of children alters the time people have for friendships. Other times a move to a new location in the same town or a change of churches causes a loss of contact.

When this happens, we have several choices. We can become bitter and resentful at fate or God for taking our friend away and resolve never to allow ourselves to be hurt again by becoming close to someone who might move away. Or, we can run up enormous telephone bills trying to keep the relationship going long distance. If the other person is still in the vicinity but clearly has other priorities, we can become aggressive, passive-aggressive or manipulative in an effort to keep the relationship the same as before.

Probably the healthiest way to respond is to realize that God gives us friendships to enrich our lives *for a period of time.* We are constantly in the process of developing friends, enjoying their company for a while, tearfully saying good-bye to many of them, and reinvesting our emotional energy in new friendships.

This doesn't mean that friends who move away are no longer friends. We may still retain rich memories of the times we spent together, and we may occasionally have special times of reunion. But the sustenance that we need from someone whom we can tangibly touch and see must be shifted to another person. If we can't accept the axiom that our friendships will constantly change, we are likely to be lonely and to live in the past.

Deepening Friendships

● Understand the facets of intimacy. Howard and Charlotte Clinebell, in their book *The Intimate Marriage,*[2] discuss how intimacy occurs, and say that each relationship is a different blend of the various kinds of intimacy. Although their book centers on marriage, nine of the ten kinds of intimacy they list can be enjoyed in any type of Christian friendship.

Work intimacy occurs between two people as they join in common projects and responsibilities, and share a mutual sense of fulfillment when those tasks have been completed. But it doesn't just happen automatically; work intimacy is felt when people cooperate together in a mutually supportive way to accomplish a project. Ken felt a bond of closeness with the two men with whom he worked in preparing for their doctoral comprehensives, as they divided up responsibilities, freely shared the results of their preparation, and passed on helpful tips and strategies.

Crisis intimacy comes from coping with a shared crisis in a mutually supportive way. When Terry and Gaye moved to a new city, they faced the emotional crisis of finding that the apartment they had leased was neither clean nor in working order when they arrived. Having neither family nor friends close by, they were forced to use all their resources as a team to deal with this unexpected and unpleasant surprise. After one week of work made the apartment livable, Terry and Gaye became aware of a special feeling of closeness—the intimacy born of coping with a shared crisis. Although they would rather not repeat that experience, the special closeness that they felt after the situation was resolved almost made it seem worthwhile.

Recreational intimacy comes from playing together, allowing ourselves to suspend our working mind-set in the presence of another person. If we constantly work we become more and more tightly wound; recreation helps us unwind. Good recreation may include a game, an engaging movie or book, or any activity in which we forget about the pressures we face in our everyday world. Without times of rest and recreation we lose our sense of humor; accomplishing work-related goals becomes all-important. Recreation (whether shared or solitary) helps us put our work-related goals in a more balanced perspective. Shared recreation helps us enjoy a fresh perspective on life.

Intellectual intimacy comes from sharing ideas with another person, feeling respected by them, and showing respect for their ideas. It involves the ability to show regard for people even when they disagree with us. This respect comes from an awareness that each of us sees only part of the truth at times, and that others may see a part of the truth that we are not seeing. People will not form an intimate friendship with someone unless they know that the other person respects their opinions and their capacity to think.

Emotional intimacy comes from sharing feelings comfortably with another person and they with you, knowing that those feelings will be respected and held in confidence. It involves the sense that someone else truly understands and cares about your experiences as a person.

Creative intimacy is the proud closeness that comes from creating something with another person. Although creative intimacy overlaps with work intimacy, creative intimacy is distinct in that it involves forming something that did not exist before. John and Toni worked together finishing off a large basement in their home and building a large wooden playground that is often the center of activity for the neighborhood children. They share a special pride and closeness because they created both things *together.*

Aesthetic intimacy comes from sharing experiences of beauty. Those experiences may be a beautiful scene in nature, a powerful thunderstorm, a beautiful musical production, or an inspiring piece of artwork.

Commitment intimacy comes when two people invest themselves in a significant altruistic cause. Two people who organize a Special Olympics event, and then enjoy the knowledge that they have benefited many lives, feel commitment intimacy.

Spiritual intimacy comes from sharing common spiritual beliefs and/or significant spiritual experiences together. Spiritual intimacy doesn't happen just because two people agree on the same doctrines; it means that those theological beliefs are experienced in some important way *in their relationship.*

Sexual intimacy is the one kind of intimacy that is to be experienced only between marital partners. Sexual intimacy is more than sexual experience; it is the mutual giving of two people to each other physically in a context of mutual caring and commitment.

How are the first nine facets of intimacy related to the deepening of friendships? For one thing, they give us an idea of some of the ways in which we can deepen our relationships. Second, they show us that intimacy is not a result of simply being with other people. Intimacy develops when we want to share that experience with the other person, to reflect upon it together. For example, a family can attend church together for many years and yet not experience spiritual intimacy. It is only as we are willing to share what is happening spiritually inside ourselves with other family members that spiritual intimacy will occur. Third, we can realize that we may develop different kinds of intimate friendships with different people.

● Dare to talk about your affections. When was the last time you told someone other than your spouse that you love him or her or that you really appreciate the relationship you have? To express affection openly is scary, for we aren't sure how the other person feels about us or how he or she will react to our expression. Especially for men, the open expression of affection occurs only rarely.

It may come as a surprise that Jesus not only openly told His friends "I love you," but also exhorted them to be equally open in demonstrating their love for each other. Here are just a few examples of Jesus' statements drawn from the closing days of His life here on earth:

A new commandment, I give you: Love one another. As I have loved you, so you must love one another. All men will know that you are My disciples if you love one another (John 13:34-35).

If you love Me, you will obey what I command. And I will ask the Father, and He will give you another Counselor to be with you forever—the Spirit of truth. The world cannot accept Him, because it neither sees Him nor knows Him. But you know Him, for He lives with you and will be in you. I will not leave you as orphans; I will come to you. Before long, the world will not see Me anymore, but you will see Me. Because I live, you also will live. On that day you will realize that I am in My Father, and you are in Me, and I am in you. Whoever has My commands and obeys them, he is the one who loves Me. He who loves Me will be loved by My Father, and I too will love him and show Myself to him (John 14:15-21).

As the Father has loved Me, so have I loved you. Now remain in My love. If you obey My commands, you will remain in My love, just as I have obeyed My Father's commands and remain in His love. I have told you this so that My joy may be in you and that your joy may be complete. My command is this: Love each other as I have loved you.

Greater love has no one than this, that one lay down his life for his friends. You are My friends if you do what

I command. I no longer call you servants, because a servant does not know his master's business. Instead, I have called you friends, for everything that I learned from My Father I have made known to you. You did not choose Me, but I chose you to go and bear fruit—fruit that will last. The Father will give you whatever you ask in My name. This is My command: Love each other (John 15:9-17).

The apostles Paul, John, Peter, and James spoke openly of their love for their brothers and sisters in Christ. They realized that love for each other was one of the distinctive ways the world would see that God had entered their lives and made a difference. If we are to follow Christ's example and His command to us, we must identify the self-talk that makes us so uncomfortable in saying "I love you" to a friend. We also must develop an awareness of how to express our affection appropriately. Here are some basic guidelines:

First, express love and affection only when you believe both people will be comfortable talking about their relationship. Christ did not begin His relationship with the apostles by saying the things mentioned above. These statements came at the end of three years of devoted companionship.

Second, don't say "I love you" as a way of forcing the other person to say the same thing back to you. Ginny complained in a counseling session that she hated to have David say that he loved her because it seemed he did this to force her to say that she loved him. He often seemed to do this when they were having difficulty in their relationship and he was trying to force her to reassure him that everything was okay. The words "I love you" should be regarded as a gift; if they're given with the intention of getting something back from the recipient, they're no longer a gift.

Third, be sensitive to the recipient's response to your statement of affection, and gauge your follow-up response accordingly. An assertive person responds from an "I count me, I count you" position. Counting the other person means considering their response before deciding how you will proceed. If the other person appears comfortable talking about the relationship, then it's appropriate to proceed. If the other person appears uncomfortable, then it's wise to defer further discussion about your relationship until the other has had a chance to assimilate what you have already said.

The fact that a person does not respond immediately to your statement of affection does not mean that he does not appreciate it or is not assimilating it. Jerry told his little sons, "I love you," when he tucked them into bed at night. Frequently they wouldn't say anything back at the time. However, during the day they would often spontaneously say, "Daddy, I love you." The seed of affection was sown in the evening, and it germinated in their minds for many hours before it produced a response. The same kind of thing can happen with adult friends.

Take the risk: Dare to tell your close friends how much their friendship means to you!

• Learn the gestures of love. Rituals are the common ways people express friendship. Every society has them, even thrives on them. Gestures of love affirm a person's feelings toward another. These significant acts say, "I care!"

Unfortunately, after being in a relationship for a while, we often discontinue caring acts that say "I love you." When this happens, some of the special feelings in the relationship begin to fade.

We can express our love through many gestures. Dr. Michael Campion has researched the gestures important to married love and has illustrated his findings in two pictorial books, *Especially for Husbands* and *Especially for Wives*. In *Especially for Husbands*, Dr. Campion reports what hundreds of wives said their husbands did to make them feel loved. Here are some of the answers wives frequently gave:

>praying together
>complimenting her in front of the children
>asking for her opinion when a decision has to be made
>helping with household work
>sending her a card that contains a tender thought
>baby-sitting so she can have a night out
>playing games with the family
>asking her for a date
>telling her she is beautiful.[3]

Dr. Campion also asked several hundred husbands what

their wives did to make them feel especially loved. Here are some of their most frequent answers:

    having a good, open conversation
    showing love to his parents
    praying for him when he is at work
    preparing his favorite food
    expressing contentment with his salary
    giving him a chance to express his frustrations when
        he arrives home from work
    listening carefully to what he has to say without
        prejudging.[4]

Many of these suggestions are valid for nonmarried friendships as well. We need to recognize the importance of everyday gestures of love and then use them to deepen the bonds of friendship.

A Note to Married Partners

Ideally, your marriage partner should be your best friend. To give that relationship maximum opportunity to grow, temporarily curtail other relationships in the early years of marriage. This allows each of you time to become secure in knowing that you are first in the other person's life.

After a few years of marriage, if you feel secure and are emotionally healthy, you will feel comfortable encouraging each other to develop friendships outside the marriage that are enriching and growth-producing.

Some marriage partners never become close friends. Sometimes a partner never lets down the walls. In other marriages, the walls may have been down at one time, but eventually unresolved conflicts have caused the walls to go back up, preventing any meaningful sharing.

Some marriage partners are unwilling to let the other one develop outside relationships because of the unconscious fear that if the spouse cares deeply for someone else, there will be less love available for him or her. If either you and your spouse is reluctant to allow the other close friendships outside your marriage, discuss the reasons for this reluctance and see what mutually agreeable resolution you can come to. The communication skills in the following chapters may help you better understand each other's perspective.

KEY IDEAS FROM CHAPTER FOUR

1. Our true wealth is found in our deep friendships.
2. An assertive lifestyle is the best basis for a deep friendship.
3. In order to develop deep friendships we must:
   – Make friendships a priority.
   – Focus our efforts on developing a few deep relationships.
   – Overcome the fear of not being accepted.
   – Take off the masks that we often wear for fear that others will reject us if they really knew us.
   – Allow time and space for intimacy to develop gradually over an extended period of time.
   – Realize and accept the fact that in today's society friendships will continuously change.
4. To understand how to deepen friendships, we need to understand the different facets of intimacy: work intimacy, crisis intimacy, recreational intimacy, intellectual intimacy, emotional intimacy, creative intimacy, aesthetic intimacy, commitment intimacy, spiritual intimacy, and sexual intimacy.

EXERCISES

Write your answers to the following questions in your notebook.

1. As you think about the five different response styles and your friendships, how would you characterize yourself— passive, aggressive, passive-aggressive, manipulative, or assertive? If you are not assertive now, or if you are assertive sometimes and nonassertive at other times, how would you like to change your external behavior so that you would be more consistently assertive?

2. Many people develop friendships of a passive-assertive variety, that is, one person is passive and the other is more assertive. These relationships may be fulfilling for both people and may last for many years because both people get some of their personal needs met through this arrangement.

• Do you think that a friendship where both people are assertive would be healthier than one where one person is assertive and the other is passive? Why or why not?

● If you are in a passive-assertive friendship, what changes could you make to help this become an assertive-assertive friendship? What resistances might you expect, either from yourself or the other person, to making this change? Do you think the benefits of the changed relationship would be worth the effort involved in making those changes?

3. A prerequisite to any friendship is that each person believes that the other person respects his or her ability to think and form opinions. Do you think that other people (especially your family) know that you respect their ability to think? If not, what changes could you make so that they would feel more intellectually respected?

4. Are you satisfied with the number and quality of deep friendships in your life? If not, review some of the obstacles to developing deep friendships mentioned in this chapter:

● not making friendships a priority,

● not making the time for deep friendships to develop,

● focusing on too many people so that there is not enough time to develop deep relationships,

● being afraid to share ourselves honestly and deeply with someone else,

● pushing the relationship to develop too fast,

● not allowing for withdrawal as well as contact time, and

● not realizing that our friends will change over time.

From the above list or from your own thinking, try to identify the obstacles that are keeping you from developing the number and quality of deep friendships you desire.

5. Identify relationships in which you experience intimacy.

● As you think about your past and present friendships, what kinds of intimacy have you experienced?

● What do you think made it possible for you to experience that kind of intimacy in that relationship?

● What kinds of intimacy would you like to be experiencing that you are not now? What could you do to develop a friendship in which that kind of intimacy would develop?

PART III

Self-Protective Assertiveness

FIVE

What Does God Say About Self-Protective Assertiveness?

If your brother sins against you, go and show him his fault.

—*Matthew 18:15*

This book explores the two sides of assertiveness: relationship-enhancement and self-protection. In the last two chapters we've discussed relationship-enhancement skills, those skills that are helpful in bringing us closer to people. The next chapters will examine self-protective skills—those skills that allow us healthy, tactful ways to

• state our own feelings, beliefs, wishes, attitudes or rights.

• disagree with someone else's point of view comfortably.

• refuse requests that conflict with our own priorities.

• defend ourselves against unfair or inaccurate accusations.

• express anger and annoyance assertively.

• deal with someone else's anger and annoyance comfortably and nondefensively.

• make reasonable requests of others.

While most Christians would agree that relationship enhancement is compatible with scriptural teaching, some of the same people believe and teach that the Bible discourages or even prohibits the use of self-protective assertive skills. They point out that we are to be humble and meek, to turn the other cheek, to prefer others above ourselves, and to give up our personal rights.

This chapter will examine biblical principles behind self-protective assertive skills. The first section will discuss bibli-

cal examples of each of the five response styles. The second
section will deal with doctrinal passages that relate to self-
protective assertiveness. The third section will suggest an
assertive process based on the teachings of Scripture.

Biblical Illustrations of the Five Response Styles

When studying Scripture, we should not expect to find the
labels *passive, aggressive, passive-aggressive, manipulative* and
assertive. Such words were not used in a technical sense until
the 1960s, when assertiveness training became popular. But a
close examination of Scripture uncovers many passages relating directly or indirectly to the five major response styles.

● Manipulation. The first example of manipulation occurs
in the opening pages of Genesis:

> Now the serpent was more crafty than any of the wild
> animals the Lord God had made. He said to the woman,
> "Did God really say, 'You must not eat from any tree in
> the garden'?"
> The woman said to the serpent, "We may eat fruit
> from the trees in the garden, but God did say, 'You
> must not eat fruit from the tree that is in the middle
> of the garden, and you must not touch it, or you will
> die.' "
> "You will not surely die," the serpent said to the
> woman. "For God knows that when you eat of it your
> eyes will be opened, and you will be like God, knowing
> good and evil."
> When the woman saw that the fruit of the tree was
> good for food and pleasing to the eye, and also desirable
> for gaining wisdom, she took some and ate it (Genesis
> 3:1-6).

Satan used three manipulative strategies in his interaction
with Eve. First, he manipulated her by creating a felt need.
Before this Eve had probably been enjoying all the good
things God had given her; now her attention was focused on
the one thing God had forbidden her. Second, Satan manipulated her by lying about the negative consequences of dis-
obeying God. Third, Satan manipulated Eve by appealing to

her desire to be as complete a person as she could be, and he falsely implied that the only way she could become complete was by breaking God's commandment.

Satan's strategies are much like those used by manipulative people today:

– They create a need (for example, the need to be loved, to be accepted).

– They suggest that the only way to meet that need is to do what they want us to do.

● Aggression. The first example of human aggression is also found in the early chapters of Genesis, in the sibling rivalry between Cain and Abel.

Now Abel kept flocks, and Cain worked the soil. In the course of time Cain brought some of the fruits of the soil as an offering to the Lord. But Abel brought fat portions from some of the firstborn of his flock. The Lord looked with favor on Abel and his offering, but on Cain and his offering He did not look with favor. So Cain was very angry, and his face was downcast.

Then the Lord said to Cain, "Why are you angry? Why is your face downcast? If you do what is right, will you not be accepted? But if you do not do what is right, sin is crouching at your door; it desires to have you, but you must master it."

Now Cain said to his brother Abel, "Let's go out to the field." And while they were in the field, Cain attacked his brother Abel and killed him.

Then the Lord said to Cain, "Where is your brother Abel?"

"I don't know," he replied. "Am I my brother's keeper?"

The Lord said, "What have you done? Listen! Your brother's blood cries out to Me from the ground. Now you are under a curse and driven from the ground, which opened its mouth to receive your brother's blood from your hand. When you work the ground, it will no longer yield its crops for you. You will be a restless wanderer on the earth."

Cain said to the Lord, "My punishment is more than I

can bear. Today You are driving me from the land, and I will be hidden from Your presence; I will be a restless wanderer on the earth, and whoever finds me will kill me" (Genesis 4:2-14).

This passage exemplifies several aspects of the aggressive response style. Generally we become angry because someone has blocked our path to a goal. In this case Cain probably wanted his sacrifice to be accepted on a par with, or given preference to, Abel's. Apparently God had already told them both how to offer an acceptable sacrifice (see 4:7), and Cain had chosen to offer a sacrifice the way *he* chose rather than the way God specified. When God accepted Abel's sacrifice and not his, Cain's goal was blocked, and he turned his anger on the person whom he thought had blocked it.

Notice that Abel didn't really block Cain from reaching his goal; Cain blocked himself. This illustrates an interesting point about sin, namely, that when we sin and cause ourselves misfortune as a result, it's very tempting to project the blame for that misfortune onto someone else, and not to accept personal responsibility for causing our difficulty.

God spoke with Cain about how to resolve his anger, but Cain disregarded God's instruction. Instead he purposely planned the first homicide, and he carried it out shortly thereafter. This illustrates another mistaken belief of the aggressive response style: Cain thought he would find happiness by taking revenge on the person whom he perceived as responsible for blocking him from reaching his goal. Aggressive people often think they will be happy if they can hurt the person who blocked them from reaching a goal, but they usually find that the enjoyment of revenge is short-lived.

When God asked Cain where his brother was, Cain not only lied ("I don't know"), but also showed callous indifference ("Am I my brother's keeper?"). God then sentenced Cain to a lifetime of wandering, never to have a permanent place to call his home. Rather than recognizing the legitimacy of God's punishment and realizing it is a reasonable consequence of his coldly calculated murder, Cain collapsed into self-pity ("My punishment is more than I can bear").

Cain's behavior is typical of those who choose an aggressive response style; when confronted, aggressive people often lie and become indifferent. Like Cain, they often end up alienated from their peer group because they fail to change or show remorse. Rather than recognizing their own responsibility in what has happened, they often resort to self-pity.

• Passive-aggressiveness. There are many examples of passive-aggressiveness in Scripture; perhaps one of the best known is the passive-aggressive complaining of the Israelites during their journey from Egypt to the Promised Land. Whenever they encountered a difficulty, rather than remembering God's powerful deliverances of them in the past, they would begin bitterly complaining about their lot. For example, as they appeared trapped between Pharaoh's army and the Red Sea, they chose to complain rather than to trust God:

> "Was it because there were not graves in Egypt that you brought us to the desert to die? What have you done to us by bringing us out of Egypt? Didn't we say to you in Egypt, 'leave us alone; let us serve the Egyptians'? It would have been better for us to serve the Egyptians than to die in the desert!" (Exodus 14:11-12)

Shortly after this the Israelites complained about the lack of fresh water (Exodus 15:24) and God miraculously provided them with the means of purifying the available desert water. Then they complained about food and God miraculously provided manna and quail (16:2-16). Later they complained again about water (17:2-7), and God provided water from the rock at Massah and Meribah. The crowning complaint happened a short time later, when the scouts came back from exploring Canaan and the people began criticizing Moses for taking them out of Egypt. They even considered stoning Joshua and Caleb, choosing a new leader, and returning to Egypt (Numbers 14:1-10). This angered the Lord so greatly that He contemplated destroying the whole nation and raising up a new nation through Moses (14:11-12).

The sin that angered the Lord so much that He would consider destroying an entire nation was their lack of faith (Numbers 14:20-38). Their passive-aggressive complaining was, in essence a complaint against God (Exodus 16:8). If the Children of Israel had assertively brought their requests directly to God in an attitude of trust, He probably would have gladly answered their needs. The Apostle Paul reminds us that the Children of Israel were guilty of three major sins that caused them to miss the Promised Land—idolatry, sexual immorality, and complaining. He indicates that the record of their travels was written to warn us not to fall into similar sins (1 Corinthians 10:1-11).

• Assertiveness. The Pentateuch also contains an example of Old Testament believers handling a potentially frustrating situation in a tactfully assertive manner—the story of the daughters of Zelophehad.

> The daughters of Zelophehad son of Hepher, the son of Gilead, the son of Makir, the son of Manasseh, belonged to the clans of Manasseh son of Joseph. The names of the daughters were Mahlah, Noah, Hoglah, Milcah and Tirzah. They approached the entrance to the Tent of Meeting and stood before Moses, Eleazar the priest, the leaders and the whole assembly, and said, "Our father died in the desert. He was not among Korah's followers, who banded together against the Lord, but he died for his own sin and left no sons. Why should our father's name disappear from his clan because he had no son? Give us property among our father's relatives."
>
> So Moses brought their case before the Lord and the Lord said to him, "What Zelophehad's daughters are saying is right. You must certainly give them property as an inheritance among their father's relatives and turn their father's inheritance over to them.
>
> "Say to the Israelites, 'If a man dies and leaves no son, turn his inheritance over to his daughter. If he has no daughter, give his inheritance to his brothers. If he has no brothers, give his inheritance to his father's brothers. If his father had no brothers, give his inheritance to the nearest relative in his clan, that he may possess it. This is to be a legal requirement for the Israelites, as the Lord commanded Moses' " (Numbers 27:1-11).

Notice the differences between how the daughters of Zelophehad handled a situation and how the Children of Israel did. The people, when faced with a difficulty, began complaining about their problem *to each other.* They never went directly to the One who could remedy it, but instead they grumbled about their lot. In contrast, when the daughters of Zelophehad experienced a situation which they believed was not right, they assertively came to Moses, the representative for God. They presented their case, confident that a righteous and gracious God would hear their request and deal with it fairly. Numbers 36 indicates that even years later, God was continuing to honor their assertive but respectful obedience.

It's interesting, especially in light of the cultural regulations of Bible times, that several of the finest biblical examples of assertiveness are women. Besides the daughters of Zelophehad we have Ruth who at the encouragement of Naomi assertively appealed to Boaz to be her kinsman-redeemer (this was in actuality a request for marriage). The implication of Scripture is that this marriage was richly blessed and honored by God. (See Ruth 3:1-9; 4:17-22; Matthew 1:1-5).

The Old Testament gives other examples of assertive women — Esther and Bathsheba. At risk to her own life Esther appealed to her husband, not once, but three times. She gained the safety of her own people and the king's permission to draft, together with Mordecai, the decree that effectively ended the threat to the Jews' existence while they were citizens of the Persian Empire (Esther 8:7-8). Likewise, Bathsheba assertively intervened with David and was successful in having Solomon placed on Israel's throne when one of Solomon's brothers tried to usurp the throne (1 Kings 1:5-40).

In Acts we see Priscilla and Aquila assertively inviting the powerful evangelist Apollos to their home and explaining to him the Christian message more accurately (Acts 18:26). The fact that Priscilla's name is always mentioned before her husband, Aquila, may mean that she had higher social standing, but it more likely means that she was the more assertive of the two. Wherever Priscilla and Aquila are mentioned, they are playing a positive role in the early church.

We see many examples of assertive courage in David's early life. He single-handedly killed both a bear and a lion when they attacked his father's flocks. He was willing to take on the giant Goliath when everyone else in the Israelite army was afraid. In each of these instances David's assertive courage rested in his faith in God: he believed that God would give him strength to do the things that were right and necessary, and so he stepped out in faith.

David also was assertive when his personal rights were violated. One example is recorded in 1 Samuel 17:17-30:

> Now Jesse said to his son David, "Take this ephah of roasted grain and these ten loaves of bread for your brothers and hurry to their camp. Take along these ten cheeses to the commander of their unit. See how your brothers are and bring back some assurance from them. They are with Saul and all the men of Israel in the Valley of Elah, fighting against the Philistines."
>
> Early in the morning David left the flock with a shepherd, loaded up and set out, as Jesse had directed. He reached the camp as the army was going out to its battle positions, shouting the war cry. Israel and the Philistines were drawing up their lines facing each other. David left his things with the keeper of supplies, ran to the battle lines and greeted his brothers. As he was talking with them, Goliath, the Philistine champion from Gath, stepped out from his lines and shouted his usual defiance, and David heard it. When the Israelites saw the man, they all ran from him in great fear.
>
> Now the Israelites had been saying, "Do you see how this man keeps coming out? He comes out to defy Israel. The king will give great wealth to the man who kills him. He will also give him his daughter in marriage and will exempt his father's family from taxes in Israel."
>
> David asked the men standing near him, "What will be done for the man who kills this Philistine and removes this disgrace from Israel? Who is this uncircumcised Philistine that he should defy the armies of the living God?"
>
> They repeated to him what they had been saying and told him, "This is what will be done for the man who kills him."

When Eliab, David's oldest brother, heard him speaking with the men, he burned with anger at him and asked, "Why have you come down here? And with whom did you leave those few sheep in the desert? I know how conceited you are and how wicked your heart is; you came down only to watch the battle." "Now what have I done?" said David. "Can't I even speak?" He then turned away to someone else and brought up the same matter, and the men answered him as before. What David said was overheard and reported to Saul, and Saul sent for him.

Apparently Eliab was jealous of David, because he had been passed over by Samuel as the Lord's choice for king. His jealousy may have intensified when David was asked to play his harp in the royal palace. When David's searching questions put him on the defensive, Eliab responded angrily by trying to put David down and telling him to be quiet.

Rather than be intimidated, David responded assertively and defended his right to speak and ask questions. He then turned away from the person who was attempting to intimidate him and continued to exercise his right to speak. Notice that even though many of David's assertive actions were based on his trust in God's strength, in other situations such as this one he was assertive because he believed he possessed certain rights as a human being.

● Passivity. David's life also illustrates another truth about assertiveness: we may be assertive in some relationships and situations and quite nonassertive or even passive in others. Probably the best-known area in which David had difficulty being assertive was in parenting, for he was very permissive. For example, there is no record that he ever disciplined his son Amnon when Amnon raped his stepsister, Tamar, and then refused to marry her as the law decreed he should. There is no record that David confronted Amnon about his responsibility to take Tamar as his wife; she apparently lived out her life in shame as a result (2 Samuel 13:1-21).

Evidence indicates that David was similarly permissive with his second oldest son, Absalom. Two years after Amnon's rape of his sister, Tamar, Absalom planned and carried out the murder of his brother (2 Samuel 13:23-29). Even though the law requiring the death penalty for premeditated murder was clear, David failed to administer justice in either his capacity as father or king. Absalom's spoiled nature is evident through many of his further actions:

– He started Joab's field on fire because Joab wouldn't come when he wanted him to (2 Samuel 14:28-30).

– He *demanded* rather than requested that he be restored to good standing with the king (14:32).

– He paraded before the people of Israel in an ostentatious and expensive manner (15:1).

– For four years he sowed discord against his father in the hearts of the people of Israel (15:2-7).

–He was willing to lead a rebellion against his own father, no matter what the cost in human lives (15:7-12).

David's son Adonijah, also suffered from a lack of parental assertiveness. Commenting on Adonijah's inappropriate behavior, 1 Kings 1:6 states: "His father had never interfered with him by asking, 'Why do you behave as you do?' "

In 1 Kings 1 we read a result of David's lack of discipline – Adonijah attempted to usurp the throne and bypass his father's right to name his successor. In a manner similar to Absalom's, Adonijah assembled chariots and horsemen and fifty runners to go before him and tried to proclaim himself king. Only the assertive intervention of the Prophet Nathan and of Bathsheba prevented the insurrection's success.

David suffered the consequences of his lack of parental assertiveness. Even though David was a man after God's own heart, and tried to lead a godly life himself (repenting when he made mistakes), he failed to enforce biblical guidelines with his children. The rape of his daughter and the deaths of three of his sons, Amnon, Absalom, and Adonijah, were all related to his lack of parental discipline.

A Closer Look at Biblical Assertiveness

Many Christians have reservations about assertiveness because a number of biblical concepts seem to be incompatible with it. They ask: As a Christian, how can I vent my frustrations when the Bible speaks against anger? Can I be assertive and still "turn the other cheek"? Aren't Christians supposed to give all their rights back to God? What about being humble and meek as Christ commanded? How can we be assertive, yet not offend our brothers or sisters in the Lord? Let's look for some answers to these questions.

• The Christian and anger. Many verses seem to command us to get rid of anger in all its manifestations.

– A gentle answer turns away wrath, but a harsh word stirs up anger (Proverbs 15:1).

– A hot-tempered man stirs up dissension, but a patient man calms a quarrel (15:18).

– Better a patient man than a warrior, a man who controls his temper than one who takes a city (16:32).

– A man's wisdom gives him patience; it is to his glory to overlook an offense (19:11).

– Do not make friends with a hot-tempered man, do not associate with one easily angered, or you may learn his ways and get yourself ensnared (22:24-25).

– A fool gives full vent to his anger, but a wise man keeps himself under control (29:11).

– An angry man stirs up dissension, and a hot-tempered one commits many sins (29:22).

Do these verses from Proverbs mean we can never be angry? If Jesus was sinless and human anger is sinful, how can this be reconciled with Mark 3:5 which recounts Jesus looking "around at them in anger, deeply distressed at their stubborn hearts"? An even more well-known example of Christ's anger is recorded in Mark:

> On reaching Jerusalem, Jesus entered the temple area and began driving out those who were buying and selling there. He overturned the tables of the money changers and the benches of those selling doves, and would not allow anyone to carry merchandise through the temple courts. And as He taught them, He said, "Is it not written: 'My house will be called a house of prayer for all nations'? But you have made it a den of robbers" (11:15-17)

Long before the words and actions of Jesus Christ were written, the Old Testament writers recorded well over 300 references to God's anger. See, for example, Numbers 25:4; 32:14; Deuteronomy 29:16-20; Judges 2:14; Isaiah 5:25.

Since God the Father and Jesus Christ are holy in all that they do, and since biblical records show both of them becoming angry, it follows that there is a righteous *divine* anger. However, whenever Scripture speaks about *human* anger, it warns us about its dangers. What is the difference?

Human anger and divine anger often differ in at least two ways: their source and their expression. God's anger—His reaction against sin and injustice—is rooted in His holy nature. In the first instance cited above, Christ was angry at the Pharisees for placing rule-keeping above compassion. In the second instance, He was angry because the temple had been turned into a place where poor worshipers were charged exorbitant prices by greedy businessmen. In both of these instances, Christ's anger was rooted in His holy nature.

Human anger often proceeds from our inability to tolerate frustration. After we have experienced a certain number of minor annoyances, we reach our limit, and the next problem makes us angry. This anger may be understandable, but its source is very different than the source of God's anger.

A second major source of human anger is that our path to a goal is blocked. When something or someone blocks our path to reaching a certain goal, we often respond with anger. Sometimes the goal we were hoping to reach is a reasonable one; other times it is based on an overly self-centered view of the situation or unrealistic expectations. In either case the human anger that comes from having personal goals blocked is significantly different from God's righteous anger.

Human anger differs from divine anger also in its expression. We express our anger by venting our frustration at the situation or by getting back at the person who blocked us from reaching a goal. Sometimes our response is far out of proportion to the situation that provoked it. While our response may be justifiable, it is expressed in damaging ways. In contrast, God's divine anger is always just and reasoned because it is bounded by His love and omniscience.

One of the most comprehensive biblical discussions of anger is found in Ephesians 4. The Apostle Paul suggests ways to put off the old style of life and to put on the new (vv. 22-

24). We are to put away falsehoods and speak only truth (v. 25), to put away stealing and work honestly (v. 28), to avoid unwholesome talk, while speaking only things that build others up (v. 29). He tells us to develop new ways of handling our anger: "In your anger do not sin," that is, don't become aggressive (v. 26a). "Never let the sun go down while you are still angry, and do not give the devil a foothold;" that is, "don't be passive" (vv. 26-27).

After dealing with other ways to put off the old way of life, Paul returns to the topic of how to effectively handle anger and frustrations: "Get rid of all bitterness, rage and anger, brawling and slander, along with every form of malice. Be kind and compassionate to one another, forgiving each other, just as in Christ God forgave you" (vv. 31-32).

These verses describe the entire range of passive-aggressive responses that occur when we suppress or repress anger: *thumos* (the outburst of anger that occurs when too many resentments have built up), *orge* (chronic anger and ill-temper), *krauge* (brawling or anger that makes sure everyone hears the grievance), *pikria* (bitterness, the emotional state that comes when we nurse grudges), *blasphemia* (slanderous, abusive speech toward an irritating party), *pasa kakis* (Paul's catch-all term for any malicious feeling not already mentioned). We are to learn how to handle frustrations without being passive, aggressive or passive-aggressive.

Other passages that speak to the issue of anger include Colossians 3:8: "But now you must rid yourselves of all such things as these: anger, rage, malice, slander, and filthy language from your lips," and James 1:19-20: "Everyone should be quick to listen, slow to speak and slow to become angry, *for man's anger does not bring about the righteous life that God desires*" (emphasis added).

Let's summarize what we've said about anger:

1. Scripture reveals a righteous, divine anger exhibited by both God the Father and Jesus the Son.

2. Scripture warns us of the dangers of *human* anger.

3. In recognizing that we will get angry (Ephesians 4:26) the Apostle Paul warns us not to be aggressive ("In your anger do not sin"), not to avoid dealing with it ("Don't let the sun go down on your wrath"), and not to let it fester (to come

out in passive-aggressive ways, vv. 31-32).

There are differences of opinion about whether the Bible teaches that there is a *human* righteous anger. Whatever view we take, we can probably agree on the following statement:

We all get angry when we face frustrations and when people block our goals, some of us more quickly and more often than others. Assertiveness gives us a method for dealing with anger-producing situations without being passive (letting the sun go down on our wrath), or aggressive, or stuffing our anger and having it come out in passive-aggressive ways at some time in the future.

The Christian's goal in assertive behavior may be different from the non-Christian's goal. The non-Christian often is assertive to get what he or she wants, albeit in a tactful way. Although a Christian may at times share this goal, *the more important goal of a Christian's assertiveness should be the restoration of relationships*. When a person does something that bothers us and the situation is not rectified, our fellowship with that person is hindered. Jesus wants us to approach that kind of situation in loving assertiveness: "If your brother sins against you, go and show him his fault, just between the two of you. If he listens to you, you have won your brother over. But if he will not listen, take one or two others along, so that every matter may be established by the testimony of two or three witnesses" (Matthew 18:15-16).

While these verses are frequently used in conjunction with church discipline, and appropriately so, the context suggests another purpose as well. The parables immediately before and after this passage discuss the process of forgiveness and restoration of relationships—both our relationship to God and our relationship to other people. Therefore, it is hermeneutically valid to use this passage as a guideline on the issue of forgiveness and restoration of human relationships.

● The Christian and nonresistance. A second reservation Christians have about assertiveness is that it seems to contradict the teaching of Jesus in Matthew 5:38-42:

You have heard that it was said, 'Eye for eye, and tooth for tooth.' But I tell you, Do not resist an evil person. If someone strikes you on the right cheek, turn to him the other also. And if someone wants to sue you and take your tunic, let him have your cloak as well. If someone forces you to go one mile, go with him two miles. Give to the one who asks you, and do not turn away from the one who wants to borrow from you.

At first glance it may seem as if Jesus is telling His followers to be passive and peaceful at all costs, never asserting themselves in any way. A closer look at these verses in their context reveals a different teaching. Just prior to this passage Jesus has been talking about how believers are to be "the salt of the earth" and "the light of the world." He has been telling them what their impact should be: they should act as moral preservatives (salt) and models of righteous living (light). Jesus' discussion of righteousness contrasted significantly with that of the Pharisees who emphasized external behavioral righteousness. True godliness, Jesus taught, includes proper internal motivation as well as proper external behavior.

Jesus then illustrated what He meant by true righteousness in several ways. Murder is not simply the act of taking someone else's life: When we harbor attitudes of bitterness and hatred toward people, we are murdering them in our minds. Adultery, likewise, is not merely an external act; it can be committed inside one's mind. If we are to be truly righteous in God's sight, we must keep our external behavior *and* our thought life pure.

Jesus then discussed another Old Testament teaching that the Pharisees were misinterpreting. When God originally gave the command "eye for eye" and "tooth for tooth" He was giving rules for Israel's judicial system. A rich man was not to be given a sentence different than a poor man; a powerful man was not to be treated differently from one who had little political power. Penalties were to be meted out without partiality and were to be proportional to the crime. However, by Jesus' time, the Pharisees had twisted the intention of this law and were using it as the basis for revenge—"If someone does something bad to you, do the same to him!" Jesus spoke out against such selfish and aggressive behavior. As the salt and light of the world, His followers were to reveal the God living within them by not repaying evil for evil.

The command to turn the other cheek was not a directive

to be followed with every relationship; if so, it would be a direct contradiction to what Jesus taught: "If your brother sins against you, go and show him his fault." Matthew 18 shows how to live assertively with brothers and sisters in the faith, how to restore broken relationships through talking out differences. Matthew 5 is an example of one way a believer can witness to aggressive unbelievers. We need not return evil for evil; but by making a nonrevengeful response, we can bear witness to the loving Christ who lives within us.

● The Christian and rights. A third concept that makes some Christians reluctant to develop assertive skills is the conviction that committed believers should view themselves as servants of Christ. Servants in New Testament times were indebted to the master who bought them from slavery, and they therefore had no rights of their own. A related teaching popular among some Christians today is that if we give all our wants, needs, and rights to God, we won't be anxious, angry, or frustrated when those rights are violated. We won't get upset because those rights don't belong to us anymore.

In contrast, most secular books on assertiveness, and some Christian books as well, insist that all human beings have several inalienable rights, and they encourage us to learn assertiveness so that we can stand up for our rights.

I believe that the Scriptures point somewhere between these two positions. Christians do have rights. God teaches in 1 Corinthians 7 that husbands and wives have rights over their spouses' bodies. Pastors have certain rights over their flock (see 1 Corinthians 9). Jesus and Paul occasionally demanded their legal rights. Although some first-century Christians gave up personal property and lived communally (Acts 4:32-35), no teaching in Scripture states that we are to give up all rights to property and ownership. This was a voluntary action on the part of the Jerusalem Christians.

The emphasis is not on exercising our rights but on honoring the rights of others. The passage in 1 Corinthians 7 is a good example. Paul did not command husbands and wives to demand their rights from each other. Rather, each was commanded to honor the rights and needs of the other. In all of our relationships, we have a right to be treated with dignity and respect as children of the heavenly King. But Scripture emphasizes our responsibility to honor those rights in others. As assertive Christians, we do not seek what we want by emphasizing our rights. We believe that a relationship is healthier if both people focus on honoring the rights and needs of the other person. We do have rights, however, and if the other person in the relationship either purposely or inadvertantly tramples on our rights or needs or feelings, the Bible encourages us to discuss this with the person.

As Christians, we sometimes choose to suspend the exercise of our assertive rights in light of God's higher calling on our lives. Our highest goals should always be to glorify God, to be an effective witness to the unsaved, and to be an agent of healing within the church. Because of these higher goals, we may sometimes choose to suspend the exercise of our personal rights. However, we *choose* not to exercise our rights. We don't give them up because we don't know how to be assertive or are afraid to be, or because we believe that we have no rights. We suspend our rights because we believe that achieving one of these goals is more important than exercising them in a given situation.

● The Christian and humility. Another resistance some Christians have to the concept of assertiveness is the belief that it's impossible to reconcile assertiveness with biblical concepts such as humility and meekness.

In Matthew 5:3 Jesus said, "Blessed are the poor in spirit, for theirs is the kingdom of heaven." In context, this probably means blessed are those who recognize the poverty of their own spiritual condition, i.e., that they cannot be saved by their own works of self-righteousness.[1]

In the same passage Jesus taught, "Blessed are the meek, for they will inherit the earth" (Matthew 5:5). The prevailing philosophy of that time was that the wealthy and powerful would inherit the earth. In contrast, Jesus taught that the true inheritors of the earth are those who recognize that we come to God, not through our own works of righteousness, but as we recognize our sin and ask forgiveness. In the millennial kingdom and throughout eternity, we shall inherit the earth. In the Beatitudes Jesus was exhorting His followers to have a right attitude toward God, themselves, and others.

Meekness is not the same as weakness. Meekness and

humility involve an attitude that enables us to be grateful for God's goodness and aware of our need of His gracious mercy. We are not to think of ourselves more highly than we ought to think, but are to recognize our need of each other; we are not to act spiritually self-sufficient (see Romans 12:3-8).

Humility is only one part of a Christian's self-concept. Other truths about who we are include the fact that we are created in God's image (Genesis 1:26), that God gave His only Son on our behalf (John 3:16), that we are adopted into the family of the King of the universe (1 John 3:1), that we are a chosen people, a royal priesthood (1 Peter 2:9). Being humble and meek does not mean we are to behave as if we had no value, worth, rights or talents. Humility means recognizing that our salvation is provided by God's grace, not by our own works; it means not having an overly inflated view of our own value and worth. And this kind of humility is not mutually exclusive of biblical assertiveness.

● The Christian and nonoffensive behavior. Another reservation that some Christians have about being assertive is their fear that assertiveness might cause them to offend someone. The Apostle Paul wrote: "Give none offense, neither to the Jews, nor to the Gentiles, nor to the church of God" (1 Corinthians 10:32, KJV).

The problem is that there are some very opinionated believers who believe that they not only have the right answers for their own lives, but also for how every other Christian should live. When we interact with such people, assertively exercising our right to think, believe, and act as we choose may cause them to be "offended." Does this mean we should nonassertively conform to their every expectation in order to be obedient to God's command?

Skandalidzo, the Greek word translated "offend" in the King James Version, more accurately means "to cause someone to stumble." What this verse is teaching in context is that when we're around weak or new Christians, we should restrict our participation in any activity that those Christians believe is wrong, in order that we not cause them to stumble in their faith. Likewise, we should restrict our freedom to do certain things around nonbelievers, if participation in those activities might prevent them from coming to Christ.

Paul's teaching here is not referring to the highly opinion-ated believer who gets "offended" by everyone who fails to conform to his beliefs of what is right and wrong. Nor does it refer to the thin-skinned Christian who gets offended by feedback about his behavior, even when that feedback is giv-en in the spirit of Matthew 18. Properly understood, then, the command in 1 Corinthians, not to offend a brother or sister or nonbeliever, is not a prohibition against the seven kinds of self-protective assertive behaviors that we've discussed in this book. It is only a prohibition against doing this in such a way that it might hinder nonbelievers from coming to Christ or believers to stumble and fall in their Christian life. *Aggres-sive behavior* might cause either of these things to happen, but *assertive behavior* is unlikely to do so.

The Bible Commands Assertiveness

● Assertiveness in parenting. Many Scriptures clearly indi-cate that we can't fulfill our role as parents unless we are willing to be assertive. For example:

– The Lord disciplines those He loves, as a father the son he delights in (Proverbs 3:12).

– He who spares the rod hates his son, but he who loves him is careful to discipline him (Proverbs 13:24).

– Discipline your son, for in that there is hope; do not be a willing party to his death (Proverbs 19:18).

– Train a child in the way he should go, and when he is old he will not turn from it (Proverbs 22:6).

The death of Eli's two sons and the judgment on Eli's house is directly attributed to Eli's passive response to his sons' sinful behavior (1 Samuel 2:12-36, and 3:13-14). We've already seen in an earlier section of this chapter that David's permissive parenting style led to the death of three of his sons.

● Assertiveness in theological and moral matters. When a church leader begins teaching things that are clearly out of line with Scripture, or when a church body begins tolerating behavior that Scripture clearly labels as immoral, Christians often withdraw from that church or denomination. What kind of response is this?

Scripture teaches that we are to be assertive whenever the congregation or denomination of which we are a part faces theological error or immorality. Here are some of the passages that speak to this issue:

– So watch yourselves. If your brother sins, rebuke him and if he repents, forgive him (Luke 17:3).

– But among you there must not be even a hint of sexual immorality, or of any kind of impurity, or of greed, because these are improper for God's holy people. Nor should there be obscenity, foolish talk or coarse joking, which are out of place, but rather thanksgiving. For of this you can be sure: No immoral, impure or greedy person—such a man is an idolater—has any inheritance in the kingdom of Christ and of God. Let no one deceive you with empty words, for because of such things God's wrath comes on those who are disobedient. Therefore do not be partners with them.
For you were once darkness, but now you are light in the Lord. Live as children of light (for the fruit of the light consists in all goodness, righteousness and truth) and find out what pleases the Lord. Have nothing to do with the fruitless deeds of darkness, but rather expose them (Ephesians 5:3-11).

– It is actually reported that there is sexual immorality among you, and of a kind that does not occur even among pagans: A man has his father's wife. And you are proud! Shouldn't you rather have been filled with grief and have put out of your fellowship the man who did this? Even though I am not physically present, I am with you in spirit. And I have already passed judgment on the one who did this, just as if I were present. When you are assembled in the name of our Lord Jesus and I am with you in spirit, and the power of our Lord Jesus is present, hand this man over to Satan, so that the sinful nature may be destroyed and his spirit saved on the day of the Lord (1 Corinthians 5:1-5).

– If your brother sins against you, go and show him his fault, just between the two of you. If he listens to you, you have won your brother over. But if he will not listen, take one or two others along, so that every matter may be established by the testimony of two or three witnesses. If he refuses to listen to them, tell it to the church; and if he refuses to listen even to the church, treat him as you would a pagan or a tax collector (Matthew 18:15-17).

– Do not entertain an accusation against an elder unless it is brought by two or three witnesses. Those [elders] who sin are to be rebuked publicly, so that the others may take warning (1 Timothy 5:19-20). [Thus we are to be assertive even against church leaders, if there is evidence that they are living lives out of harmony with Scripture.]

– It was He [Christ] who gave some to be apostles, some to be prophets, some to be evangelists, and some to be pastors and teachers, to prepare God's people for works of service, so that the body of Christ may be built up until we all reach unity in the faith and in the knowledge of the Son of God and become mature, attaining to the whole measure of the fullness of Christ.

Then we will no longer be infants, tossed back and forth by the waves, and blown here and there by every wind of teaching and by the cunning and craftiness of men in their deceitful scheming. Instead, speaking the truth in love, we will in all things grow up into Him who is the head, that is, Christ (Ephesians 4:11-15).

– [An elder] must hold firmly to the trustworthy message as it has been taught, so that he can encourage others by sound doctrine and refute those who oppose it (Titus 1:9).

Clearly it would not be wise or appropriate to assertively challenge our pastors each time they say something we think is not quite right. When a person speaks without verbatim notes, sometimes ideas will come out unclearly or imperfectly. Also, there is room for legitimate differences of theological opinion, and we should not demand that our pastor agree with us on every point. What these verses are pointing out is that if any Christian, leader or layperson, engages in unbiblical moral conduct or begins to teach or preach doctrines that are clearly incompatible with Scripture, then we are not doing our biblical duty if we passively tolerate this or passively withdraw from that church. We have a God-given responsibility to encourage, and if need be, exhort one another.

The Process of Assertiveness

Let's examine a few verses from Ephesians 5 to understand more clearly how assertiveness can operate. It's not clear whether Ephesians 5:21, "Submit to one another out of reverence for Christ," is part of the previous paragraph (5:15-20), in which case it applies to all believers in their relationship to each other, or whether it is part of the following paragraph (5:22-24), in which case it would apply primarily to husbands and wives relating to each other. Either way, this verse is relevant to the issue of how we are assertive.

The Greek verb used in Ephesians 5:21 for submitting to each other has three possible voices: *active*—I do something to someone else; *passive*—Something is done to me; and *middle*—I do something to myself. In Ephesians 5:21, "submitting" is in the middle voice. The passage does not point to something I make you do or to something you make me do, but to something *each of us does to ourselves*. Our submission, then, is an action we choose to take.

As Christians, our assertiveness should not demand but appeal. If two people are living in mutual submission, they will respond to that appeal by meeting it or by working out a compromise resolution that respects the needs, feelings and rights of both. Each of us should ask (appeal to) the other person to be sensitive and responsive to our needs.

The following six-step procedure can help us learn to handle frustrating situations in an assertive manner:

● Stop the angry impulse before it comes out. (Proverbs 14:16-17, James 1:19). There are at least two important reasons for doing this. First, if we let angry (aggressive) words come out of our mouths or if we engage in aggressive behavior, damage is likely to be done to our relationships with others, even if we say we're sorry later. It's much better to prevent the damage from ever being done than to have to repair damage after it has been done.

Second, the angry expression of anger makes us angrier. Many people believe that Freud taught that it was healthy to ventilate anger. A more accurate statement of Freud's belief was that it is unhealthy to repress anger (that is, not deal with it in some way). To say that it is unhealthy to repress anger is not the same as saying that it's healthy to express it aggressively.

Think for a moment about a time when you were frustrated and vented your anger aggressively. Immediately after venting your anger, were you more angry at the person than before you started or less so? Aggressively venting our frustration often intensifies angry feelings. Aggressive expression of anger causes our bodies to secrete adrenaline into our bloodstream, and the adrenaline intensifies angry feelings.

It's not good to *repress* angry feelings either. The following steps explain how to deal with frustrating situations without resorting to either aggression or repression.

● Identify the goal that has been blocked. One of the simplest ways to understand where anger comes from is the *frustration-aggression hypothesis,* developed by John Dollard in the 1930s. Briefly, this theory states we are constantly moving toward some goal. For example, our goal may be to arrive at work on time, to get a raise or promotion, to have our children do well in school or to behave in a civilized manner when we have company. When someone or something thwarts us from reaching that goal, we feel anger toward whatever or whoever we believe is responsible for blocking our path. Whether we express that anger depends on how much danger we perceive there will be if we express our feelings.

Dollard's frustration-aggression hypothesis was anticipated centuries ago in the pages of Scripture. James stated it like this: "What causes fights and quarrels among you? Don't they come from your desires that battle within you? You want something but don't get it" (James 4:1-2).

Sometimes we may not even be aware of what goals are blocked and are making us feel frustrated. The next chapter will help us become more aware of subconscious goals that, when thwarted, make us feel frustrated.

• Decide whether the blocked goal is important enough to talk about. Sometimes after identifying your blocked goal, you decide that it's not crucial that you reach it. By letting go of your goal, you also let go of the anger produced when someone blocks you from reaching it.

Other times after identifying what your blocked goal is, you'll realize that it's based on an unrealistic expectation. By replacing that unrealistic expectation with one that is more realistic, you are likely to find that your anger will diminish.

Still other times after identifying your blocked goal, you'll realize that it's based on an overly self-centered view of the situation. As in the previous two categories, if you can let go of your overly self-centered goal and replace it with another goal that counts the needs of yourself and others, you'll find that your anger will diminish.

• If you decide your goal is a legitimate one, communicate it to the other person. A model for doing this, called the Triple-A Model of Assertiveness, will be presented in chapter 7, along with specific information on how to communicate your needs, feelings and goals most effectively.

When the other person in the relationship is an unbeliever, you may decide that it is more important to not say something that might offend him or her (and therefore not create a stumbling block that might impede the person's reception of the Gospel), than it is to express your legitimate assertive rights. However, if you approach a situation with healthy assertiveness, you probably will not offend, and may even cause the other person to respect you more because of your ability to stand up for yourself in a nonaggressive way. But as Christians we should be willing to suspend the exercise of our assertive rights if we think it might increase the chances of us being an effective witness to an unbeliever.

When the other person in the relationship is a believer, we should decide whether failure to discuss the blocked goal will damage the relationship. If not discussing the problem will cause us to withdraw from that person out of hurt or anger, then in obedience to Christ's command we should take the initiative to talk with the person and try to resolve the situation (Matthew 18:15-17). If we know another has hurt feelings because of something we have done, even if we're convinced we didn't do anything wrong, we should seek them out and attempt to be reconciled (Matthew 5:23-24).

• Find out the other person's goal. After you have said what you'd like, make sure to ask the other person what he or she would like, particularly if that person is nonassertive and wouldn't tell you unless invited to do so. If the other person is *very* frustrated, it may be wise to ask what he or she would like first, and then explain your goal. The reason for this is that a frustrated person is more likely to listen to you if he or she believes you've carefully listened first.

• Try to work out a compromise. "Each of you should look not only to your own interest, but also to the interests of others" (Philippians 2:4). In Ephesians 5:21 we read, "Submit to one another out of reverence for Christ." These two verses, among others, form the theological basis for finding mutually acceptable resolutions when two people have goals that conflict with each other. A healthy resolution is one that is made from the stance of "I count me, I count you." Chapter 9 will discuss various workable compromises.

KEY IDEAS FROM CHAPTER FIVE

1. The Bible contains many examples of the five response styles.

2. Assertiveness can help us obey the command of Ephesians 4:26 because it gives us an alternative to passivity, aggression, or passive-aggression.

3. Christian assertiveness is compatible with "turning the other cheek," humility and meekness, and the command to "not cause someone to be offended," when these concepts are properly understood.

4. It is not true that the believer has no rights. However, the scriptural emphasis is on making sure we honor the rights of others, rather than on demanding our own.

5. Biblical parenting requires that parents be assertive. Scripture records the unhappy results of nonassertive (i.e., permissive) parenting.

6. When a person or a church either begins to tolerate

immorality or preach unbiblical doctrines, we are commanded to respond to that situation with assertion rather than with passive withdrawal.

7. Six steps for handling anger assertively are
 – Stop the angry impulse before it comes out.
 – Identify the goal that has been blocked.
 – Decide whether the blocked goal is important enough to talk about.
 – If you decide your goal is a legitimate one, communicate your goal to the other person (appeal, don't demand).
 – Find out the other person's goal.
 – Try to work out a compromise.

EXERCISES

Write your answers to the following questions:

1. Eight basic tenets of an assertive philosophy of life have been summarized in the following way:

• By trying to govern our lives so as not to ever hurt anyone, we end up hurting ourselves and other people.

• If we don't tell other people how their behavior affects us, we are denying them an opportunity to change.

• We all have a right to express ourselves, as long as we don't violate the rights and dignity of others.

• Sacrificing our rights usually results in training others to mistreat us.

• Not letting others know how we feel and think is a form of selfishness.

• There is more to be gained from life by being free and able to stand up for ourselves and honoring the same rights in others.

• When we are assertive, everyone involved usually benefits.

• When we do what we think is right for us, we feel better about ourselves and we have more authentic and satisfying relationships with others.[2]
 – With which of these tenets do you agree?
 – With which would you disagree? How would you modify them and why?
 – Which tenets do you have most difficulty applying?

2. Manuel J. Smith in *When I Say No I Feel Guilty* lists an assertive "Bill of Rights." The following is a summary of rights he believes each person has.

● You have the right to judge your own behavior, thoughts, and emotions, and to take the responsibility for their initiation and consequences upon yourself.

● You have the right to offer no reasons or excuses for justifying your behavior.

● You have the right to judge if you are responsible for finding solutions to other people's problems.

● You have the right to change your mind.

● You have the right to make mistakes—and be responsible for them.

● You have the right to be independent of the goodwill of others before coping with them.

● You have the right to be illogical in making decisions.

● You have the right to say, "I don't understand."

● You have the right to say, "I don't care."[3]

– Which of these do you think are consistent with biblical Christianity?

– Which do you think are inconsistent with a Christian faith? Why?

3. From the thoughts in exercises 1 and 2, from Scripture, and from your own thinking, draw up your own assertive philosophy of life.

4. What mistaken belief caused David to be so permissive with his children, even though he was a godly man?

5. If you realize that you've not been an assertive parent, what do you think you've been saying to yourself consciously or subconsciously to keep yourself from being assertive?

6. If a brother or sister in the Lord sins against you, do you usually use the procedure found in Matthew 18 to work the situation through with them? If you do not, what do you think you've been saying to yourself either consciously or subconsciously to prevent yourself from using this process?

7. Are there any theological points in this chapter with which you disagree? Identify why you disagree.

S I X

Self-Awareness:
A Prerequisite to
Self-Protective Assertiveness

Speaking without thinking is like shooting without aiming.
—*Old Proverb*

Everyone has felt the frustration of being irritated about something but not knowing why. We sometimes don't understand our negative feelings or why we have them. Minor irritations can become walls between us and other people. Especially in close relationships, small frustrations can combine until eventually two people become distant, and feelings of love no longer exist. Self-awareness—the ability to get in touch with our thoughts, feelings, and goals—is a prerequisite to being assertive with others. Assertiveness—the ability to talk about things that bother us in a loving way—is necessary so that we do not become alienated from others we love.

Many factors prevent us from identifying our thoughts, feelings, and goals. First, we often lose touch with our emotions because we have repressed them. Children are often disciplined for angry behavior—whether it's jealousy toward a sibling or frustration toward a parent. Often neither parents nor children make distinctions between identifying angry feelings versus acting out aggressive or disrespectful behavior. It's important to help children learn to express angry feelings in a respectful manner rather than to suppress all negative feelings. Children who get repeated spankings for negative emotions or anger will eventually learn to repress these feelings automatically.

Similarly, adult experiences often reinforce our tendency to

112

suppress and repress negative emotions. When we are angry, jealous, or depressed, we sometimes hear, "Snap out of it," or "Get with it." While it's not healthy to focus our attention *constantly* on thoughts that produce negative feelings, it's important to get in touch with these feelings so that we can deal with them in healthy ways. As children and adults, we're often told that all negative feelings are unhealthy. Because of this, we unconsciously assume that we should keep them out of our awareness.

A second cause of low self-awareness can be rooted in religious training. Biblical teaching and preaching may *seem* to forbid us from acknowledging such emotions as anger, jealousy or fear. The next logical step is to believe that Christians should never experience anxiety. The same goes for honestly recognizing emotions of anger or jealousy or lust; we come to suppress those feelings so constantly that they are repressed; that is, they are suppressed out of our conscious awareness without any recognition that they were even there. As a result, our awareness is lowered and our emotions are never or rarely discussed. Men particularly tend to be out of touch with their emotions.

The Importance of Heightened Awareness

It's important to be in touch with our feelings, especially as they relate to other people and conflicts we have with them.

If we identify what we feel, we can do something to change feelings that need to be altered or reversed. If we look at the cause of those feelings, either we can change our thinking—if we realize that the feelings are coming from unrealistic or overly selfish expectations—or we can develop an assertive action plan, if that is called for.

Whether or not we are consciously aware of our emotions, they *do* affect our behavior. When we are aware of our feelings, we have a greater degree of control over how we express them. If we are unaware of them, they may come out in ways we don't intend. When Zelda was a child she was often punished for expressing her anger. Her mother was very concerned about correct appearances; any sign of disrespectful behavior from her children angered her greatly, and resulted in vigorous discipline. Zelda's mother was not aware of the distinction between *recognizing* anger and *inappropriately expressing* anger. Consequently she punished both, causing many of Zelda's feelings to go underground.

Zelda has brought into adult life three unconscious assumptions: other people will mistreat you; bad things will happen if you express your feelings honestly; it's best to bury your feelings of anger and frustration.

Because of the first unconscious assumption, Zelda sometimes reads mistreatment into other people's behavior when they're not intending to harm her. Because of the other two assumptions, she doesn't tell them what she's thinking and feeling. However, her hurt and anger often come out in unintended ways: She sometimes withdraws from people or is short with them. Other times her anger comes out in nonverbal ways, like the lack of a smile when she greets them or a cold edge to her voice when she talks to them. Others interpret these passive-aggressive behaviors to mean that either she is angry with them or doesn't want to be their friend. Zelda's unconscious assumptions prevent her from relating to these potential friends in healthy ways and from being fully aware of her own thoughts and feelings.

Daniel continually refuses to think about things that bother him. As far as he's concerned, when you think about a problem you encourage it to grow bigger. Daniel's inner turmoils from the many unresolved tensions and issues partially repressed in his subconscious mind have caused him an ongoing variety of psychosomatic illnesses.

Both Zelda and Daniel are living with the mistaken belief that self-control means concealing negative emotions. Neither realizes that when emotions are suppressed or repressed they don't go away—they go underground and may come out in ways over which they have *less* control. Both could be living happier lives of self-control if they would identify their negative emotions and then deal with them.

Dimensions of Awareness
There are at least five important components of our internal awareness. These components are:
senses ➝ thoughts ➝ feelings ➝ intentions ➝ actions.[1]

- Senses. Our awareness of an event usually starts with one of our five senses. We see a frown on a friend's face. We hear words spoken softly. We feel a light touch on our shoulder. We smell the aroma and taste the sweetness of a favorite dessert. Sense data is usually not self-interpreting. Our senses simply observe, experience, and describe. To understand what our sense data mean, we must supply an interpretation.

- Thoughts. Our interpretations or thoughts are based on our hunches, expectations, and beliefs about what the sense data means. We usually evaluate sensory data based on assumptions made from our own past, present, and anticipated future experience. For example, Amy has had several experiences in which her close friends abandoned her without explanation. Now whenever a friend shows any kind of negative emotion in her presence, Amy interprets this to mean that this friend is angry with her and is about to reject her as others have. Sometimes the person is not angry with Amy at all, but Amy interprets the person's behavior in light of her own past experience.

Our interpretations of the meaning of the sense data we are receiving may be right or wrong. We may conclude that a person who is crying is sad or distraught. However, the person may be crying because she is happy or relieved. Similarly, the frown on a friend's face may not mean he's angry. It may mean that he has a headache, is having difficulty concentrating, or is formulating what he wants to say next.

In a relationship, two people can easily misinterpret the meaning of the other's behavior. Many hurt feelings and disagreements are based on what we *think* someone meant rather than on what the other person truly intended.

For example, Harold works third shift at the textile mill— 11 PM to 7 AM. His wife, Mary, works from 8 AM to 5 PM in an attorney's office. Each morning the couple has half an hour together before Mary leaves for work. Lately, just to catch up on the news and to have music in the background, Mary started listening to the radio while getting ready for work and eating breakfast. Within a few days of this, Harold began avoiding her, reading the newspaper when he got home from work and watching more television on weekends. Mary interpreted this to mean that Harold liked the newspaper and television more than he liked her.

Both Harold and Mary interpreted their partner's behavior to mean something different from what was intended. Harold assumed that Mary preferred listening to the radio over talking with him. Hurt, he turned to the newspaper and television to occupy the time he used to spend with her. Mary interpreted his actions as rejection. During a discussion about this chain of events, Harold found out that Mary wanted the music as *background* for their time together, not as a *replacement* for it. He was able to let go of his hurt feelings and anger, and no longer needed to express his feelings by withdrawing to the television. Once Mary understood the reasons for his withdrawal, she was also able to let go of her interpretation that he didn't want to have anything to do with her and of the hurt that she had felt.

● Feelings. Our feelings are any combination of emotions we may have in a given situation. It may be very difficult to identify specific feelings because we sometimes have more than one emotion at the same time; for example, we may simultaneously feel angry and afraid.

The following feelings are but a partial list of emotions that affect us—singularly and in combination—every day.

affectionate	determined	hopeful	sad
afraid	discontented	hopeless	satisfied
alarmed	discouraged	horrified	sexy
angry	eager	hurt	strong
ashamed	ecstatic	impatient	stumped
anxious	elated	insecure	surprised
bewildered	embarrassed	irritated	sympathetic
bored	enraged	jealous	talkative
burdened	envious	joyful	tender
bushed	excited	lonely	tense
calm	fearful	loving	terrified
carefree	frustrated	mixed up	thankful
cautious	glad	nauseated	thrilled
close	grateful	panicky	timid
comforted	grief-stricken	peaceful	torn

compassionate	grumpy	pleased	unloved
confident	guilty	proud	upset
confused	happy	relaxed	uptight
contented	hateful	relieved	weepy
depressed	hesitant	resentful	zealous

Paul and Wanda's teenage daughter, Dana, was supposed to have been home from a date at 11 PM. By 12:30, her parents were filled with anxiety, certain that tragedy had befallen her. When they heard a car drive up, both parents felt a combination of relief and anger. Within Paul's self-awareness were all of the following thoughts and feelings:
– Thank God you're home safely!
– We really love you!
– Why didn't you obey us?
– Don't you understand the agony this puts us through when you don't come home on time and don't call?

What angrily came out of his mouth was: "Why weren't you home when you were supposed to be?" Dana, who had a reasonable explanation for being late, heard only her father's anger. She immediately thought her parents were unloving, too possessive, and totally devoid of understanding. Unless someone in the household is able to communicate the underlying love that produced the frustration, the relationship between Dana and her parents will be at least temporarily disturbed.

We can change our feelings by gaining new, more accurate sensory data or by reexamining our interpretations of the sensory information. For example, Al is standing in line when suddenly someone bumps into him from behind, almost knocking him over. Al's immediate feeling is one of anger and frustration at what he interprets to be carelessness. Al's feelings and interpretations change, however, when he turns around and sees the man who bumped him wearing dark glasses and holding a white cane. Al's angry feelings weren't changed by ignoring the situation or by suppressing his anger. His feelings changed when he gained more data and was able to alter his interpretation of the incident.

How can we heighten our awareness of our feelings? How can we begin to get in touch with inner feelings if we have been suppressing or repressing our awareness for many years? Here are four possible ways:

1. Notice natural physical cues our bodies give. Our bodies often act out our feelings, even if we have repressed our conscious awareness of those feelings or if we are focusing on the task at hand and therefore not paying attention to those feelings. If you are speaking in a public meeting and are focusing on what you want to say, you may notice that your voice sounds tense, even though you are not aware of being tense. In other kinds of situations, you may find yourself scowling or tightening your muscles, without being aware that you are frustrated. You may be tired or depressed, but you may not be aware of this until you realize you are slumping in your chair. By paying attention to the natural physical cues your body shows, you may be able to get in touch with feelings you would otherwise miss.

2. Pay attention to body language or to nonverbal signals we send. Body language is somewhat similar to physical cues, but many physical cues are totally internal and no one is aware of them but ourselves. Body language is more external and visible to others. For example, if while talking to someone we fold our arms, the other person may think we are communicating, "I don't agree with what you're saying," or "I'm not sure I agree with what you're saying, and I'm suspending judgment until I've heard more and had time to think it over." Folded arms may also mean something different from either of the above. Since there are no universally accepted interpretations of nonverbal behavior, we can't be dogmatic about what other people's nonverbal behavior means. However, it is helpful for us to pay attention to *our own* nonverbal behavior and use it to become aware of thoughts and feelings going on in our subconscious mind.

Jennifer's attention to her own nonverbal behavior helped her understand some subconscious attitudes she held. She became aware that whenever a serious or conflicting issue was brought up, she would almost always finish her statements with a little laugh that was often not appropriate to the content of what was being discussed. As she analyzed this, she realized that her family had always dealt with conflict in unhealthy ways that often caused a good deal of pain. Now whenever she heard a statement which could lead to conflict, she would emit a nervous laugh that was saying two things: "I'm uncomfortable with conflict because I'm afraid it will erupt into a painful dispute," and "Maybe if I laugh about it, I can reduce the seriousness of this situation, and nothing bad will happen."

3. Ask a situational question: It's often a helpful exercise to ask yourself questions such as "What am I feeling right now?" "What happened (sensations) and how did I interpret those sensations to make me feel that way?" Sometimes the situation won't allow you to take the time to do that during the event itself, but you can do this afterward and gain important insights about why you were feeling the way you were.

4. Try to share those situational feelings with another person. When something is bothering you and it seems that your attempt to process it inside your own head just ends up going in circles, it may be helpful to talk through the situation with a good listener. Occasionally John would be in a staff meeting at his business and something would occur that left him feeling either uncomfortable or with the thought that there was some "unfinished business" that needed his attention. He would sometimes share his thoughts and feelings with his assistant. Often just the process of sharing helped him clarify the situation. At other times his assistant's perspective on what occurred provided more sensory data or another interpretation of the event, and helped clarify what happened and what, if anything, needed to be done.

It's important to be aware of the differences between thoughts and feelings. We often say "I feel" when we are actually describing a thought. If we start a sentence with "I feel that . . ." (as opposed to "I feel . . .") we are actually describing a thought but calling it a feeling. While this may seem like a technical distinction to make, it's very important as a basis for understanding ourselves and communicating effectively with others. Notice the difference between the following:

Thought: "I feel that you don't love me anymore."

Feeling: "When you spend almost all your spare time watching television rather than with me (sensations), it makes me think that you like the TV more than me (thoughts), and I feel hurt and lonely (feelings)."

● Intentions. We also must learn to be aware of our intentions—what we want to happen or what we want to do in a specific situation. A person may have varying kinds of intentions, desires, or goals:

— Immediate: "I want to eat lunch now."

— Medium range: "I want to lose twenty pounds by my birthday."

— Long-term: "I'd like to become a millionaire within ten years."

— Open-ended or broad: "I want to be loved and appreciated."

— Specific or narrow: "I would like to start jogging two miles a day, three days a week."

As with feelings, we may have more than one intention at a time, and our intentions may conflict with each other. For example, one part of us may want to express our frustration about someone's behavior; another part of us may not want to risk expressing our frustration to the other person.

Our intentions or desires are sometimes hard to pinpoint. Here is a list of some relatively common intentions.[2] In any situation we might want to:

avoid	disregard	persuade
be accepted	exploit	play
be friendly	explore	praise
clarify	help	reject
conceal	hurt	share
demand	ignore	understand

A proper understanding of our intentions is vital to self-awareness. Our desires or wants propel us to action. Based on our sensations, thoughts, and feelings, we choose what we want to do and then we act. For example, Dodie sees Bill frowning—her sensation. Her thought, "Bill is angry with me" causes her to feel anxious, because she *wants* Bill to be happy with her. Dodie's anxiety relates to her goal of having a positive relationship with Bill, and she interprets Bill's frown as an indication that her goal or intention is not happening. When something blocks our path to a goal we often become angry. We can also become frustrated when we have two goals and fulfilling one may block us from fulfilling the other. For example, George wants to "take it easy" this semester at college, but he also wants to graduate *summa cum laude* and be accepted at Harvard Law School. He will continue to be frustrated until he identifies his two conflicting goals and decides how he will resolve the conflict.

To become aware of this part of our self-awareness we must ask ourselves, "What do I want right now?" When we're frustrated, it's often helpful to ask, "What goal got blocked?"

Sometimes we pursue a goal we're aware of and find we're frustrated because pursuit of the first goal is blocking a second goal that we're not fully aware of. For example, Tom was asked to play *Monopoly* with his wife and son after supper one evening. He wanted to spend some pleasant time with Barbara and Timmy (a goal), so he agreed. After forty-five minutes of playing, however, Tom found himself becoming increasingly irritated about the length of the game. After thinking about what was causing his irritability, Tom realized that it was caused by a conflict of intentions. While he wanted to spend some pleasant time with his wife and son (one goal), he also wanted to make a few important telephone calls and to read some notes for a board of directors meeting the next morning (another goal).

What can Tom do now that he realizes that his anger is being caused by mutually incompatible goals? He can choose to reach one goal and let go of his desire to reach the second goal. If both goals are important, he can try to find a workable compromise that would allow him to reach both goals, either fully or partially. For example, he may decide that he can make his telephone calls and prepare for the board meeting as long as he stops playing *Monopoly* by 8:30. He can talk over his decision with Barbara and Timmy and relax and enjoy the time with them until 8:30. Or he may choose to explain the situation to Barbara and Timmy, pull out of the game then, do his work, and then spend some time with them the next evening. Either way he would be reaching both of his goals, and he would be preventing frustration from spilling over and keeping him from reaching *either* goal.

Sometimes we say that we want to do a certain thing, but then we never reach that goal. This *may* be an indication that we have two goals: the one we verbalized and a second unspoken one. For example, we may say that we want to get up each morning and have a half hour of personal devotions, but rarely do it. The second, hidden goal—that we want to stay in bed for an extra half hour—conflicts with our first goal.

The same kind of pattern may prevent us from breaking bad habits (smoking, eating too much, watching too much television, spending too much money). Although we want to break the habit—one intention, we also want the pleasure that comes from the habit—a conflicting intention. We make a choice about which goal is more important to us at the time, and our actions indicate which goal we give higher priority to.

Internal conflict because we have two mutually incompatible goals can cause us to feel irritable, and we may displace our irritation on those around us, even though they may not be causing our frustration. *Displacement* means that anger coming from one situation or person is vented onto another situation or person. Whenever we feel angry it's important to identify where the anger is coming from.

If our anger is arising from two mutually incompatible goals that are both our responsibility, it's unfair to displace that irritation onto others.

If the anger is coming from two mutually incompatible goals, one or both of which are partially or fully under the control of other people, then we need to decide whether the goal that is being blocked by them is a valid and important goal. If it is, then it is appropriate to talk with them about how their behavior is blocking our goal. We also want to invite them to tell us their goals, so that the resolution can consider the goals of both individuals (see Philippians 2:4).

● Actions. Actions include both our words and our behavior. Sometimes our words will be inconsistent with our behavior—that is, we'll say we want to do one thing, but we'll actually do something else. This is because our words represent one aspect of our thoughts, feelings, and intentions, but other thoughts, feelings, and intentions may override the ones about which we spoke. For example, Judy said that she wanted to quit being sarcastic with her husband, an intention, and she was honest in what she said. However, when a difficulty arose between them, she often reverted to her passive-aggressive ways. She was as frustrated about this as was her husband. Judy eventually realized that when there was a conflict, her desire to win the argument or to get back at her husband overrode her desire to quit using her old tactics. It was only as she began using self-talk, telling herself that maintaining a good relationship with her husband was more important than winning a particular argument, that she started to make her behavior at home consistent with her stated goal.

At first the difference between *intention* and *action* can be confusing, especially the difference between intention and future action. Intention indicates a *desire* to do something—I would like to make better grades. Future action goes a step further and implies a commitment to action—I will study at least four hours a day every day except Sunday.

The Five Dimensions of Self-Awareness

Sensing → Thinking → Feeling → Intending → Acting

Whenever we analyze the various components of our self-awareness, we will be most effective if we focus around a single issue at a time. Without clearly defining the issue, our minds or discussions often wander from one issue to another, but fail to clarify or resolve any of them. It's easy to be overwhelmed if we don't stay focused on one issue at a time.

When working toward self-awareness, we may focus on issues such as making a career change, resolving a disagreement at church, sharing the household work, making a financial decision, disciplining a child, or handling a problem at work. The following situations will allow us to see how the dimensions of awareness can be used to increase our self-awareness before discussing an issue with another person. The various dimensions of awareness are connected, with one leading to another. Remember that we won't always think or talk about issues in sequence from sensations to thoughts to feelings to intentions to actions.

● Situation one. Bill White, a successful business executive and trusted church leader, returned to his office after attending an out-of-town seminar:

On his desk Bill notices a message from his pastor: "Bill, please call about something important. We need to talk." The message was thirty-six hours old.   *Sensation*

Bill says to himself: "But Marcy [his secretary] didn't tell me of this message when I called in yesterday."   *Thought*

Bill feels *anger* at Marcy for not relating the message and *chagrin* because the pastor trusts Bill to respond quickly to difficult situations within the church.   *Feeling*

Bill says to himself: "I certainly don't want the pastor to think I am negligent."   *Intention*

Bill decides: "I'm going to call Marcy in and let her know how dissatisfied I am with her for not getting this important message to me."   *Future action*

Bill sees his well-organized desk.   *Sensation*

He remembers how prompt and efficient Marcy usually is.   *Thought*

He feels remorse about his anger.   *Feeling*

Bill wants to maintain a professional and caring relationship with his secretary.   *Intention*

Bill remembers: "The few times I have blown my stack at Marcy, I was wrong."   *Past action*

Bill reminds himself: "Her decisions have been correct in the past. If she made a mistake, then I owe her the benefit of the doubt."   *Thought*

Bill sees the message again.   *Sensation*

Bill says to himself: "But I have to get back to the pastor."   *Future action*

Bill continues: "I want to make sure he thinks I'm dependable."   *Intention*

Bill decides: "The best thing to do is call the pastor and apologize for the delay in responding. I'll tell him that my secretary failed to give me the message because she was so busy handling other details while I was out of town."   *Future action*

Bill dials the church telephone number.   *Present action*

Bill was able to process his sensations, thoughts, feelings, intentions and plan his actions before talking to his pastor or his secretary. By spending time thinking before acting, he was able to identify and accomplish his goals of maintaining a good relationship with his secretary and communicating to his pastor his desire to be responsive to him and to the church's needs.

At first Bill moved through his dimensions of awareness in a left-to-right sequence: from *sensations*, to *thoughts*, to *feelings*, to *intentions*, and then to *actions*. As he understood his situation better, he focused on certain parts of his self-awareness until he was able to resolve the conflict between his desires to maintain his good relationship with his secretary and his reputation as a responsive church leader.

Let's look at a more complicated situation where *three* intentions seem to conflict with one another.

● Situation two. Mary, a middle-aged homemaker, works in an attorney's office as a secretary. Her husband works in a textile factory.

Mary wants to go back to college part-time and eventually earn a degree in accounting.   *Intention*

Mary also desires to maintain her home in a neat and orderly manner for herself, her husband, and her two grown children who still live at home.   *Intention*

Mary wants to continue to work full-time at the attorney's office because the family needs the income.

Intention

The day she got off early from work and went by the college admissions office to get an application, she arrived home to the "normal" scenario—dirty dishes in the kitchen sink, soiled clothing waiting to be washed, pizza crusts left behind on the coffee table by her adult children, and her husband sitting in front of the television.

Sensation

Mary feels disgust, anger, and hurt.

Feeling

Mary says to herself: "I wish everyone would do their share to keep the house clean and picked up."

Intention

Mary continues: "But I already know what will happen if I ask for help. My husband has never helped me, and my kids behave just like he does."

Thought

She says to herself: "It's not fair."

Thought

Mary feels self-pity.

Feeling

Mary continues: "If all of us are adults and all of us want to benefit from living in this home, then it's only fair that we all pitch in and share the work."

Thought

Mary decides: "I'm going to make up a list of chores needing to be done in order to keep the house clean, and a list of what I think is a fair division of labor. I'll present this to the family and be open to their input. However, if they're not willing to help me with some of the work, then I'll do what I think is my fair share of the work and leave the rest undone."

Future action

She continues: "That may make it a bit unpleas-   *Thought*
ant for a while, and I may need to adjust to a
messier house, but it's impossible for me to
work full-time, go back to college, and do all of
the housework. Even though I don't like the
prospect of this, I think it will be better for me
in the long run than indefinitely postponing going back to college."

She says to herself: "I don't want to cause hard   *Intention*
feelings, but I also don't want to train my family
to believe that every bit of housework is my
responsibility."

She decides: "I will take the risk and be asser-   *Future*
tive with them, even though it won't be easy."   *action*

Overcoming Fear of Sharing Your Inner Self

This chapter has focused on becoming aware of your inner
experience as a prerequisite to sharing your thoughts, feelings and intentions assertively. You can't communicate effectively if you don't know what you're feeling and why. At this
point you may be aware of some fear in sharing information
about situations that bother you. Here are some of the reasons people often have some apprehension at this point:

● You may be aware of negative feelings you have suppressed or repressed. That's not uncommon. If you have
been in a relationship for several years, the other person may
have developed a number of habits that frustrate you, particularly if you're nonassertive or easily intimidated.

● You may be a little alarmed at the intensity of your
negative feelings. If you believe that Christians should not
have intense negative feelings about anything, you may feel
guilty about the feelings you are becoming aware of.

● Because of past incidents when you tried to be assertive,
you may be afraid of how the other person in the relationship
may respond if you speak honestly of your feelings or desires. You may be fearful of starting a heated argument.

The above feelings are normal and are probably part of
what has kept you from being assertive in the past. Don't try

to initiate self-protective assertiveness based on what you've learned in this chapter unless you're dealing with a very receptive and responsive partner. In the coming chapters you'll learn more about *how* to be assertive. Use the exercises to lay the groundwork for this assertiveness.

KEY IDEAS FROM CHAPTER SIX

1. Many of us have low self-awareness because of parental discipline, because of statements we have heard throughout life that encourage suppression or repression of feelings, and because of religious training.

2. If we repress our awareness of feelings, those feelings may get acted out through our behavior in ways that damage our relationships or our testimony for God.

3. Becoming aware of our feelings gives us more control over changing those feelings that need to be changed.

4. Becoming aware of our thoughts, feelings, and intentions is a prerequisite to being able to talk about them.

5. The dimensions of self-awareness include sensations, thoughts (or interpretations), feelings, intentions (or goals), and actions.

6. Two common sources of frustration are blocked goals and having mutually conflicting goals, where reaching one goal thwarts us from reaching the second one.

7. Processing our self-awareness prior to a conversation with someone else can often help us interact in a healthier manner than if we immediately react to the situation.

EXERCISES

Write your answers to the following questions:

1. Do you agree or disagree with the author's contention that it's important to help children learn to express angry feelings in a respectful manner rather than suppress all negative feelings? If you agree and have children, how do you think you should alter your present ways of responding when your children express negative feelings?

2. Try to identify any subconscious beliefs that keep you from developing awareness of your thoughts and feelings?

Where do you think you picked up such beliefs?

3. Do you agree or disagree with the author's statement that when strong emotions are suppressed or repressed they don't go away, but only go underground and come out in ways over which we have less control? Why or why not?

4. Can you think of a time when you were quite frustrated about something and then were able to let go of that anger? What happened? Did you develop a new interpretation of the situation? Did you decide that your blocked goal wasn't that important, and let go of your goal?

5. Think of a time when you had two conflicting goals at the same time? What were they? What did you do?

6. Read through the list of feelings on page 116. In your notebook make three columns. In the first column write ten feelings you are most often aware of in everyday situations. In the second column write ten emotions you are the least aware of or that you seldom experience. In the third column list five to ten emotions which you have the most difficulty either acknowledging or knowing how to express (some of these may be the same ones you listed in columns 1 or 2). What do you think makes it more difficult either to acknowledge or to express these particular feelings?

7. Reflect on a particularly puzzling, painful, or frustrating situation that happened during the past few days. Write one or more answers to each of the following questions:

● What did you *sense?*

● What did you *think?*

● What did you *feel?*

● What were your *intentions* in the situation?

● What *actions* did you take—mentally, verbally or nonverbally?

8. When thinking about a problem, do you find that you often let your mind drift from one issue to another without concluding the first? Do you think this is a good mental habit and way of resolving problems? Why or why not?

9. When discussing (or arguing) about an issue with someone else, do you find that you often move from one issue to another without resolving the first? Does this generally help or hinder the process of resolving the first issue? Why?

SEVEN

The Triple-A Model
of Assertiveness

One's philosophy is not best expressed in words, it is expressed in the choices one makes. . . . In the long run, we shape our lives and we shape ourselves. The process never ends until we die. And the choices we make are ultimately our responsibility.

—Eleanor Roosevelt

Potential for conflict exists in every relationship. The cause of most conflict can be understood in the following way: Each of us has certain needs or desires—to feel secure, to feel significant, etc.—that cause us to move toward related goals or intentions. Often we are not consciously aware of these goals until someone blocks our path toward them or fails to meet our expectations. When another's behavior doesn't match our expectations, or when a person's behavior blocks us from reaching our goal, we become frustrated. Conflict can easily result.

Gordon and Jean have been married for several years. One of Gordon's needs is to be respected. He had always unconsciously believed that a wife who really respects her husband would not disagree with him about important issues. Jean had unconsciously recognized her husband's belief and had usually given in to him whenever she realized that he felt strongly about something.

Recently, however, Jean has strongly disagreed with the rules Gordon has set for their twelve-year-old daughter and with the way he is disciplining her. Jean's desire to protect her daughter and give her a healthy environment are so strong that she has begun to assertively disagree with Gordon. Her behavior has blocked him from reaching one of his goals, that of feeling respected by a wife who never disagrees with him. His attempt to intimidate her back into "submission" causes her to recognize another unconscious goal of her own—having a voice in shaping the rules for and discipline of their children. Conflict ensues.

The causes of this conflict can be understood at two levels. At a surface level the conflict is caused by a difference in opinions about childrearing. At a deeper level, the conflict is caused because Gordon's unconscious goal or intention—to be respected—is thwarted by Jean's intention—to have a voice in deciding how to raise their children. In order to resolve this conflict completely, Gordon and Jean will have to work out a resolution on both levels.

How do you decide when assertiveness is appropriate? Do you use assertiveness whenever you're frustrated about something? Let's review the six steps for handling anger assertively from chapter 5 to help in answering those questions.

- Stop the angry impulse before it comes out.
- Identify the goal that has been blocked.
- Decide whether the blocked goal is legitimate and important enough to talk about.
- If you decide that your goal is a legitimate and important one, communicate your goal to the other person. Appeal, don't demand.
- Find out the other person's goal.
- Try to work out a compromise.

Use the third step to determine whether or not to assertively discuss a situation. Sometimes you will be frustrated, but after identifying your goal, you will realize your goal was based on an overly selfish or unrealistic expectation of the other person. By letting go of the expectation, you can also let go of the frustration that occurred when that goal was blocked. At other times you will realize that although the expectation was realistic, it wasn't that important. In this case you'll also be able to let go of your goal as well as your frustration at not reaching it.

Generally, a blocked goal should be talked about if you believe that it is important and it is based on what you consider to be fair and realistic expectations of the other person.

Gordon and Jean's disagreement fit these two criteria.

Once you have decided that your goal is important enough to talk about, you need a method that will minimize defensiveness in the other person and will maximize the chances for successfully resolving the issue. The goal of this chapter is to give you such a method.

The Triple-A Model of Assertiveness

Sometimes self-protective assertive statements include only a single word, "No!" or a single sentence, "I would prefer not to spend Saturday afternoon cleaning out the garage." When we assertively state our conclusion without stating the reasons for coming to that conclusion, others may view us as curt, selfish, or unwilling to compromise. For example, when Ken's wife asked him to help her clean the garage on Saturday afternoon, he realized he couldn't do it. He could simply say no, or he could take the time to explain: "I know that the garage needs cleaning, but I promised Jonathan and Benjamin (their two sons) that I would make them new wooden swords on Saturday afternoon, and I think it's important to keep that promise." Obviously, his refusal would be met with more understanding if he took the time to explain.

In general, when we are being assertive with people we care about, it is best to give longer statements that explain more about our thoughts and feelings. Such statements may use the same format that we employ in everyday conversation; however, at times it may be helpful to have a format especially designed for situations that require assertiveness.

One such plan I have called the Triple-A Model of Assertiveness, where the three A's are an acronym for its three component parts: Affirmation, Assertion, and Action.[1]

For example, Jim and Sharon Carpenter both work full time. A few months ago Sharon assertively discussed with Jim her frustration that she was doing seventy-five percent of the work around the house even though both of them spent equal amounts of time working outside the home. Jim was not excited about the prospect of doing more work around the home, especially since in his family it had been considered "women's work," but he eventually saw the validity of Sharon's points.

For the last two months, Jim has been helping Sharon more, but she isn't happy with one part of the arrangement. As a result she spends some time identifying her thoughts, feelings, and intentions. Then she prepares the following triple-A script and arranges to meet with Jim to discuss this issue. When the appointed time arrives, she says:

Affirmation: "Jim, I want you to know how much I appreciate your help with the housework since we talked two months ago. I imagine that it probably hasn't been easy for you to do some of the things that you've done, and because of that I appreciate your help even more. I'm also happy that you've kept up your part of the bargain without my having to complain or remind you of what to do. I appreciate all you've done." (Jim nods.)

Assertion: "There is one thing that's bothering me though, and I wanted to talk with you about it before it does further harm to our relationship. What I'm referring to is that the last two or three times we've been out with other couples—the party at the Wilsons', the Bible study a couple weeks ago, and the after-church social last Sunday night—I overheard you talking about how you were helping out in the kitchen and cleaning the house.

"When I heard your comments I felt uncomfortable because I was concerned that some of the men or women who heard you might believe I was lazy or domineering and that that was the reason you were having to help with the housework."

Action: "I appreciate your sharing the family work, and don't want to in any way discourage that. What I would like to ask is that you not make comments in public about how much work you do around the house. If you'll discontinue making public comments about the work you do, I'd appreciate it a whole lot. I'll also try to 'brag' about you when it would be appropriate in our conversations with other couples."

● Procedure-setting. Before we look at each of those components, note that an important step in conflict resolution lies in setting a time to talk with the other person about the situation. When an important issue needs to be resolved, it's best to alert the other person about it. Ideally, this will open the conversation with a shared positive intention—an agreement to discuss the issue.[2]

Common sense indicates that the worst time for discussions is when one or both people are tired, upset, or psychologically unprepared. Granted, some books tout "winning through intimidation," that is, winning by being much more prepared than the other person. Surprising the other person may enable you to gain an immediate goal, but only at some expense to the relationship, since it operates from an "I count me, I don't count you" framework. True consideration in procedure-setting means finding and agreeing to a time when both people will be psychologically rested and will have had adequate time to think through their thoughts, feelings, and intentions.

Suggest a specific time when both you and the other person will be psychologically rested and emotionally prepared to discuss the issue. It is not always necessary to make an appointment beforehand, especially if you're dealing with a relatively small issue; however, procedure-setting becomes more important in a potentially tense situation, or when the issue may require clear heads and time for considerable discussion.

You can suggest a setting in a very casual manner, such as "I would like to talk with you about _____. Is tonight after dinner okay with you?" With that statement, you place importance on the other person's time and feelings, and also instill the idea that what you discuss will be mutually important. Agreeing to discuss the issue and setting a mutually acceptable time to do it are two important first steps in resolving conflict.

Let's take a closer look at the three components of a Triple-A script.

● Affirmation. One of the dangers of many earlier assertiveness training programs has been the assumption that people will naturally respond positively to self-protective assertiveness. At least two sets of experiments have raised questions about this assumption. In an experiment by Hull and Schroeder[3], male and female college students responded to a female confederate (someone playing a predesigned role) who behaved either passively, aggressively, or assertively. The students then rated the confederate on an adjective rating scale. Hull and Schroeder found:

On the adjective rating scale, in addition to being seen as fair, assertive, nonrevengeful, and friendly, assertive behavior was also seen as dominant, unsympathetic, and aggressive. On several measures ... responses to assertion and aggression were similar. These results suggest that assertiveness training needs to be concerned with more than the effectiveness of an assertive response. If an assertive response is evaluated as aggressive, dominant, and unsympathetic, the relationship with the person asserted against may be damaged (p. 27).

Woolfolk and Dever[4] conducted two experiments whose findings were consistent with the Hull and Schroeder results. In the first, 255 college undergraduates read and reacted to three different typescripts of persons being spoken to passively, aggressively, or assertively. For each situation and response style, the students were asked to rate the personality and behavior of the speaker and the feelings of the recipient. The researchers found that:

– Assertive behavior was viewed as significantly kinder than aggressive behavior but considerably less kind than passive behavior, and

– Assertive speakers were seen as less hostile than aggressive speakers, but more hostile than passive speakers.

In a second experiment, ninety-six undergraduate college students listened to audiotapes portraying a situation in which an individual's work and peace of mind were disrupted by an excessively noisy stereo blaring from an adjacent apartment. Four types of responses were made to the offender: Passiveness, Aggression, Assertion I–standard assertiveness, and Assertion II–assertion plus extra consideration. Assertion II was further described as "a response in which the offended party made a special effort to acknowledge the needs of the other and be friendly and polite while at the same time requesting that the stereo be played softer."

The main findings of this experiment were:

– Standard assertiveness was rated as more polite, less neurotic, less hostile, and more satisfying to the recipient than aggression, but more hostile and less satisfying to the recipient than passiveness.

– Assertiveness plus extra consideration was rated as significantly less hostile than either aggressiveness or standard assertiveness.

– Standard assertiveness and assertiveness plus extra consideration were rated as equally effective in causing behavior change in the offending party.

– Passivity and assertiveness plus extra consideration both left the recipient feeling equally satisfied, and both of these conditions were much more satisfactory to the recipient than either aggressiveness or standard assertion.

At least one assertiveness trainer has criticized these findings on a number of grounds. They examine such a small number of possible real-life situations that it is invalid to generalize from them and conclude that assertiveness plus extra consideration is always better than standard assertiveness. Second, these are role-played situations, and so the results may not be representative of what would happen in real life. Third, the subjects are college students, and their responses may not be typical of the general population.

However, until we have evidence to the contrary, these research studies do suggest that we put extra consideration or affirmation into our assertiveness statements whenever we are being assertive in a relationship that is important to us. By prefacing our critical or self-protective feedback to someone with affirmation, we reduce the chance of the person believing that *he* or *she* is being rejected, rather than a specific behavior.

Affirmation can include both a beginning statement mentioning one or more positive behaviors for which you appreciate the other person, as well as additional affirming statements interspersed throughout the assertive statement. For example, you can mention the positive feelings you have toward the person. You can share your desire that the relationship continue to be a positive and mutually satisfying one. You can affirm your belief in your partner's good intentions. You can affirm previous efforts they have made, even if those efforts have not been completely satisfying to you. Your tone of voice and your nonverbal behavior when speaking to them can convey affirmation. Your goal should be to include enough affirmation so that the other person knows that while you are unhappy with some aspect of his or her behavior, you still love and respect him or her as a person.

When you are frustrated with someone, you may not feel very positive toward that person at the moment. It might seem false, even hypocritical, to make an affirming statement to them. It may seem that the only honest thing to do would be to vent your frustration.

However, when you do this, you are often not expressing the whole truth either. Often, in addition to the frustration you are feeling about a specific situation, you have positive feelings toward the person and a positive desire to remain friends. Although you may not be strongly aware of those feelings at that precise moment, they are nevertheless part of the total reality of your relationship. Therefore it's not dishonest or hypocritical to affirm your positive desires for a good relationship, even though that may not be the strongest emotion you are feeling at the time.

In their book *Beyond Assertiveness*,[5] John Faul and David Augsburger express their belief that for Christians, affirmation of the other person should be an important part of assertion. They summarize their thoughts in the following way:

> Affirmation is Primary.
> Assertion is Secondary.
>
> Love before leveling.
> Trust before risking.
> Care before confronting.
> Support before criticizing.
> Understand before interpreting.
> Empathize before advising.
> Affirm, then assert.

It's also good to include affirming or encouraging statements throughout your conversations on a daily basis. If you use encouragement only as the first step in an assertive statement, people will tense up whenever you affirm them because they'll wonder what's coming next.

Are there times when affirmation should not be used in an assertive statement? While there are no empirically based answers to this question, we might hypothesize that affirmation should be used cautiously or bypassed in the following situations:

–When you have no past relationship with a person, and therefore little basis to make an affirmation statement. (Note, however, that in Woolfolk and Dever's second experiment, affirmation plus extra consideration was rated more positively than standard assertion even when both persons were strangers to each other.)

– When the person you are talking to is very manipulative, and therefore might use any affirmation you give them as a basis for discounting your assertive request.

– When you are so frustrated with the person that any affirmation would come out in an ungenuine way. (However, in this case it may be wise to wait until your anger has cooled before trying to be assertive.)

● Assertion. After you have affirmed the person with whom you feel a conflict, describe the specific behavior that causes you frustration. Good assertive statements try to minimize accusations, since accusations usually result in the other person becoming defensive. You can reduce defensiveness in three different ways.

– The first way is to make "I statements" rather than "you statements." "I statements" identify your personal sensations, thoughts, feelings, and intentions, while "you statements" assume that you know what is happening within the other person's mind. "You don't really love me" is a "you statement." "When you do _____, I think you don't like me" is an "I statement." The first statement assumes that the speaker can read the receiver's mind; the second statement reports the speaker's feelings. "I statements" are better than "you statements" because most of us are annoyed or become defensive when someone uses "you statements."

"I statements" identify your feelings without accusing the other person; conversely, "you statements" appear to blame the other person. "When you do _____, I feel hurt" will be received much more readily than "You make me feel angry."

Let's look at a situation as it would sound using either "I statements" or "you statements." Suppose Brenda has prepared a delicious meal, even spending extra time on her husband's favorite dessert—a Boston cream pie. She eyes the clock as it approaches 6:00, Curt's expected arrival time. By 7:00 she has a massive case of jitters combined with anger. When Curt finally opens the front door, part of the dinner is no longer beautiful or edible. Brenda is obviously frustrated and very disappointed.

"You statements" by Brenda might be very direct and to the point: "You inconsiderate @#$%¢*! You can cram this Boston cream pie in your ear, for all I care. You could have at least called to say you'd be late. Make your own supper from now on!"

Even though Brenda might feel justified in making numerous angry "you statements," if her primary intention in the relationship is to maintain a lasting marriage, her purpose would be better served by making "I statements": "I'm glad you arrived safely, but I understood that we were going to have dinner at six. I'm disappointed that we'll not be able to enjoy it much since the food is overcooked and dried out. I feel hurt and angry that I had to wait for so long without hearing a word from you that you'd be late."

– A second way to reduce a person's defensiveness is to describe what you would like changed in terms of *specific behaviors* rather than in terms of *personality characteristics*. Instead of saying, "I don't think you love me," keep your statement focused on specific behaviors: "When you go for several weeks at a time without saying 'I love you' or holding my hand, I start to wonder if something is wrong."

Instead of "You don't care . . . " you might say, "I hear you saying that you love me, but when you don't spend much time with me, it *seems to me* that you have very little love for me." Instead of an employee saying to a supervisor, "You make unreasonable demands on your staff," the employee might say: "I feel very pressured when you tell me that you want me to do three or four extra assignments each week in addition to my normal responsibilities. Usually my normal responsibilities keep me going as fast as I can."

– A third way to reduce a person's defensiveness is to avoid generalizations such as "never" or "always." A statement such as "When we were first married, you often did little things that said 'I love you.' It seems to me that for the last month or so you have stopped doing most of those things," will be better received than "You never do anything to show me that you love me."

As you work to avoid or reduce conflict by describing situations that bother you assertively, you can see how important it is to be able to identify and describe the sense, thought, feeling, and intention dimensions of your awareness. The more specifically you can describe what you sensed—saw, heard, touched, tasted, or smelled—the more clearly you can discuss a situation. Sense statements describe what, where, when, who, and how. As you describe what you have sensed, you can discern whether or not your interpretations are plausible: "I heard you say . . ." or "This morning I saw you. . . ." The more specifically you describe your interpretations or thoughts, the easier it is for other people to indicate whether or not your interpretation is different from their intended message. A good description of their behavior may also help them become aware of emotions that have been repressed out of their conscious awareness.

For instance, when Sam and Arlene first tried to talk together, it was obvious that something was amiss. Arlene was fairly certain that Sam was angry, but when she asked what he was angry about, he denied having such feelings. Finally she said, "Sam, you say that you aren't angry, at least consciously so, but here are some things that make me believe something is bothering you. When you came home you didn't kiss me as you usually do. You went to the bedroom, changed your clothes, then went straight to the living room and began reading your *Sports Illustrated* without even saying hello to me. If there's something bothering you, I would really like you to tell me what it is so we can discuss it."

By describing the sensory data that was causing her to interpret Sam's actions as anger, Arlene gave Sam an opportunity to reexamine his own feelings and either agree with her or give an alternative explanation of his behavior.

As mentioned earlier, a common mistake regarding feelings is to label a thought or interpretation as a feeling. If you hear yourself saying: "I feel *that* . . . ," you'll usually be describing a thought or an interpretation. Also, effective feeling statements are generally more personal than thought statements: "I feel very secure and loved when I'm with you," rather than "We're a great couple, aren't we?" Effective *feeling* statements are not clouded by opinions, evaluations, or questions.

The assertion phase always includes a statement of the other person's behavior that is bothering you. Depending on the relationship you have with the person, you may or may not decide to share the feelings prompted by their behavior. Usually in close relationships it improves the other person's ability to understand why it is important for them to change their behavior if you share your feelings.

When Martha and her husband came home from a Christmas party, she complimented him on how handsome he looked that evening. She then described an offending behavior and expressed how she felt: "However, I felt hurt when you spent most of the evening talking with Shirley and left me unattended in a large group of people I don't know." (Note: Often *hurt* underlies feelings of anger. In most instances, it's better to share the underlying feeling of hurt, as Martha did, than to share the resultant anger.)

Sometimes it's best to describe the person's offending behavior without expressing your feelings. Three kinds of situations may warrant withholding your feelings: commercial relationships (business, employer/employee) where the primary emphasis is on providing a service and only secondarily on the service-provider's feelings; estranged relationships where the other person may not care how you feel or may even delight in making you feel bad; and with strangers, where the other person has little concern about how you feel. Expressing your feelings during the assertion phase of an assertive statement is primarily useful in situations where the other person cares enough about how you feel to be motivated to change a behavior that is causing you pain.

• Action. To briefly review, the first section of an assertiveness statement should affirm the other person. The assertion phase should describe the behavior that bothers you. The action phase should indicate how you would like the behavior to change. Generally the "action" line should be the mirror image of your "assertion" line. That is, if you have identified an annoying behavior, your action line would request that the behavior stop. If in your "assertion" line you have indicated that the absence of a certain behavior bothers you, your action line would ask that it begin.

Assertion: "I feel frustrated because you seem unwilling to discuss this topic."

Action: "I'd like a commitment from you that we will discuss it and try to work it through to some sort of acceptable resolution or compromise."

— or —

Assertion: "I feel frustrated because you've promised to fix the broken window as soon as you have time, and yet you've spent the last three weekends watching television and have made no movement toward fixing it."

Action: "I don't want to become a nag. However, I would like a definite commitment from you as to when you will fix the window."

As you can see, your "Action" line is an expression of your desire or goal.

When you are identifying a desired action, remember to make a request or an appeal, not a demand. Our human nature is much more likely to agree to a behavior that is requested rather than demanded. This holds true for all relationships, including parent/child and employer/employee. If we treat others with respect, they will usually want to respond to our requests. Save demands for extreme situations.

Negotiation may be necessary, so be open to alternative suggestions to your "action" line. Sometimes the other person may agree to your specified requests exactly as you asked for them, but at other times a person will have needs or goals that conflict with yours. Healthy, mature adult relationships involve give and take. A person who always insists on having his or her own way is being aggressive—(I count me, I *don't* count you)—rather than assertive. Chapter 9 will deal more fully with negotiation techniques.

It's wise to include a time frame indicating an acceptable starting or ending point for the requested change. Otherwise you may be in the frustrating position of having an agreement whose completion is postponed again and again.

Always consider what is fair and possible for the other person. If your daughter has average intelligence, it's hardly fair or reasonable to specify that she bring home a straight-A report card. Likewise, if your husband is having to work hard to provide necessities for the family, it's hardly fair to ask him to buy you an expensive luxury item.

Applying the Triple-A Model

Assertive self-protective skills can be broken down into seven categories. These include the ability to:

    – state your own feelings, beliefs, wishes, attitudes or rights.

    – disagree with someone else's point of view comfortably.

    – refuse requests that conflict with your priorities.

    – defend yourself against unfair or inaccurate accusations.

    – express anger and annoyance assertively.

    – deal with someone else's anger nondefensively.

    – make reasonable requests of others.

Let's look at some examples of using a Triple-A Model of Assertiveness in several of these categories.

● Standing up for your own feelings, beliefs, wishes, attitudes, or rights. The situation: You bought a pair of expensive slacks at a clothing store in the mall, but when you got home, discovered a significant flaw. You have driven back to the store, walked to the mall through a sudden rainstorm, and discovered that the store has a policy of no returns. An assertive script might go something like this:

Affirmation: (Speaking to the manager or whoever is acting as manager at the time): "I've shopped at your store for several years, and have always enjoyed the fine quality of your merchandise. I've recommended your store to several of my friends."

Assertion: "I'm shocked to learn that you have a policy of no returns, even when the merchandise is clearly imperfect. I can understand that restocking and bookkeeping fees cost a store considerable time and money, and I realize that some people abuse the privilege by sometimes returning merchandise without a satisfactory reason" (This is affirmation, because it shows empathy for the other person's position). "But I think it's unreasonable for you to make a blanket statement of no returns, especially when the merchandise is clearly flawed."

Action: "I'm returning these defective slacks and would like to exchange them for a nondefective pair or for a refund."

• Refusing requests that conflict with your priorities. The situation: You've been asked by the nominating committee of your church to run for the position of deacon. Your first assertive response is to ask for a few days to think about the nomination, rather than immediately saying yes, as you once did.

After talking this over with your family, you receive a consensus from them that they'd like to see more, rather than less, of you. Your response to the nominating committee might go something like this:

Affirmation: "Thank you for the honor of being nominated for deacon. I know the importance of being willing to serve the church in this way."

Assertion: "However, recently I've become aware of the importance of spending more quality time with my family. After discussing this matter with them and thinking it over, I've decided to say no to any further time commitments that would take me away from them."

Action: "Therefore, I'm declining the nomination. Thank you for considering me, and I wish you well in finding suitable candidates."

• Dealing with someone else's anger. Jesus said, "If you are offering your gift at the altar and there remember that your brother has something against you, leave your gift there in front of the altar. First go and be reconciled to your brother; then come and offer your gift" (Matthew 5:23-24).

Suppose you are teaching a Sunday School class. A few weeks ago one of the members, Jim, volunteered an opinion with which you disagreed. You tried to express as tactfully as possible your alternative opinion and the reasons you held it. However, you noticed that Jim left as soon as the class was over and has been attending another class ever since. He also seems to be avoiding you during church services.

You prepare what you'd like to say, then pray for an opportunity to talk with Jim. None comes for a few weeks, and Jim's avoidance behavior continues. Finally you call his home and ask him to call you when he is free in the evening. Your assertive message might go like this:

Affirmation: "Hello, Jim. Thanks for returning my call. How are you?" (listen to his response) "How is your family?" (listen to his response)

Assertion: "Jim, something happened a few weeks ago, and I'm concerned that it may have offended you. Do you remember our discussion about _____, and how you and I saw things differently at one point? Since that time I've missed you in Sunday School and also at church.

"I feel sorry if I handled the discussion in a way that offended you, or if I've done something else that offended you. As a brother in the Lord, I don't want anything to be unresolved between us.

Action: "If there's anything I've done that has caused you to be irritated with me, I'd like you to let me know, so that we can talk it out." (pause to let Jim respond)

If Jim is angry with you and admits it, you can work toward resolving the issue. If he's not angry with you but changed classes for other reasons, you can feel reassured that there's no rift between you. If he's angry but refuses to admit it, your initiative in trying to resolve the difficulty may help him let go of his resentment.

● Making reasonable requests. The situation: Julia is working full-time, but her husband and two grown children still expect her to do most of the housework. Her children, nineteen and twenty-one, are living at home while they attend college. Julia is working to help pay for their college expenses. Julia has called a family meeting.

In your notebook write a simple script for her, requesting help in taking care of the housework. After completing your script, compare it with this sample:

Affirmation: "I appreciate the fact that you are loving and appreciative of me. The birthday party last night was wonderful."

Assertion: "However, it's getting to the point that I'm unable to do everything that you expect of me here at the house *and* do my job well at work. Each of us has a full-time job outside the home, but I'm expected to do all the housework.

"I think this is an unfair situation. I've asked you to meet together because I'm frustrated that you have not helped me unless I have asked you."

Action: "I've made a list of the major jobs that benefit the whole family and how much time each takes per week. What I propose is that each of us volunteers for jobs that represent one-fourth of the total work hours. Then every month or two we could have the option of making trades.

"If you're willing to go along with this plan or with some other plan for fairly dividing the work, I'll continue to work outside the home to help with your college tuition.

"If you're unwilling to help with the household work, I'm unwilling to continue to do two full-time jobs. I will do the majority of the household work if you choose not to help me, but I will resign from my outside job and you will be responsible for finding the money for college costs. You may decide which of these two options you prefer."

Putting the Scripts to Use

How do you use the Triple-A Model? I suggest the following process. When you have a situation that is bothering you, use the dimensions of self-awareness to understand why it is bothering you. Sometimes you will find that your frustration is caused by someone blocking a goal of yours, but as you think about it, you realize your goal is unrealistic or overly self-centered. By letting go of the goal, you will also release the anger that is caused by having the goal blocked.

If you find that your frustration is caused by someone blocking a goal which seems to you to be both important and reasonable on your part, write out what you would say using the Triple-A Model of Assertiveness.

If your attitude about the matter does not change after a day or two, ask the other person to agree to a time when you can talk over the matter. Go over the script several times in your mind so that you have memorized the important points. Then talk with the other person about the situation, without using your notes. Talking without notes will make the conversation feel more natural and comfortable for both of you.

KEY IDEAS FROM CHAPTER SEVEN

1. Conflict is a normal part of a relationship because inevitably each person's activity will sometimes block the other person from reaching one of their goals.

2. As people become more healthy and self-confident, the number of conflict-related discussions may actually increase (at least temporarily) because both people feel comfortable telling the other when one of their goals is being blocked.

3. A six-step procedure has been suggested for handling conflict assertively rather than aggressively.

4. Sometimes we can be assertive with only a single word ("No!"), but frequently it is good to explain more fully what we would like and why.

5. Assertive statements may use the same language and structure that a person uses in their regular conversations, or may sometimes use a format specifically developed to help them be assertive.

6. The Triple-A Model of Assertiveness is one such model and has three components: affirmation, assertion, and action.

EXERCISES

Write your answers to the following questions:

1. Jim and Monica are a reasonably happily married couple, with one thorny problem. Jim enjoys watching sports every weekend, and he spends many hours on Saturday and Sunday glued to the TV set. As a "football widow," Monica regularly

has felt every possible negative emotion and has on occasion expressed some of them.

This coming weekend, however, she has determined to assert herself wisely, and has begun to consider several positive, constructive "I statements" for the situation she will undoubtedly face. Help Monica come up with "I statements" that could be used in the affirmation, assertion, and action components of an assertive statement.

Jim's intentions are in conflict. He wants to relax and watch his favorite teams play, but he also desires to let Monica know that he considers their marriage relationship more important than television. Write some "I statements" Jim could use to convey his conflict of "wants."

What solutions could count both Jim and Monica?

2. Use what you've learned about writing assertive scripts to answer the following questions:

• Think back to a recent time when someone gave you critical feedback that harmed your relationship. Try to remember what that person said. Use what you have learned in this book as well as your own experience to identify what made their feedback aggressive rather than assertive.

• Think back to a time when someone gave you critical feedback in a positive, helpful way. Try to remember what that person said. Identify what positive assertive elements that person incorporated into their feedback.

3. Most of us have had the experience of trying to be assertive about something and then becoming aggressive in the process. Try to identify one or two situations in which this has happened to you. Can you identify what behaviors caused you to become aggressive, even though your intention was to be assertive? How could you have changed that interaction so that it would have remained assertive?

4. Look back in your notebook to your answers to questions three and four at the end of chapter 2. Using the Triple-A Model, write out scripts for those areas you identified in which you would like to be more assertive.

EIGHT

Responding to Detours

The more active and fruitful your life, the more you will receive criticism.

—Author Unknown

A young boy went pheasant hunting for the first time. In preparation he and his father had spent hours shooting at stationary targets and tin cans. Out in the wilds, however, the boy's success was less than he had hoped. Noting his son's growing frustration, the father asked, "What's the matter?"

The boy angrily replied, "It's not like it was when we practiced at home. Out here the targets keep *moving* all the time!"

If you have been nonassertive or passive for years and suddenly begin making assertive statements, others may not be prepared for the new you. They may even decide that they liked the passive you better and may attempt to detour you back into your nonassertive ways.[1] When they don't respond to your carefully prepared assertive statements in the way you had anticipated, you may feel like the boy who was learning how to hunt, "Out here the targets keep *moving* all the time!"

This chapter will explore some ways people may use to try to detour you or keep you from maintaining an assertive stance. This is where many people fail in their attempts to become assertive. Short courses on assertiveness can teach you how to make initial assertive statements, but the real test of assertiveness is whether you are able to ward off attempts to detour you back into nonassertiveness. This chapter will discuss several techniques to use in conjunction with the Triple-A Model to maintain an assertive lifestyle.

You may find that if your style has been aggressive, passive-aggressive, or manipulative, you will not meet with much resistance as you develop an assertive lifestyle. The people around you will find your affirming, assertive lifestyle to be much more pleasant than an aggressive, passive-aggressive or manipulative one. However, if your style has been passive, you may meet with a lot of resistance to becoming assertive. People used to a passive person living life from an "I count you, I don't count me" position, may resist the new "I count you *and* I count me" stance.

Being assertive and maintaining assertiveness will help you develop the qualities that the Apostle Peter recommended—self-control, perseverance, and brotherly kindness (2 Peter 1:5-7). The ability to make initial assertive statements and to maintain an assertive lifestyle is important if you are to enjoy healthy relationships and have good feelings toward your brothers and sisters in Christ.

Responding to Others' Assertiveness and Criticism

When someone is assertive with you, you may respond in the same way you would if the person had criticized you: in both situations the person is asking you to consider some information (about yourself or about what you are doing) that initially you may not want to consider. For that reason responding to assertion and responding to criticism are considered together in this section.

If you want others to be open to your assertiveness or your criticism, you must respond openly when others are assertive or critical with you.

Think back to a time when you closed yourself off from constructive criticism. Take the time to describe the situation in your notebook. Then write out the answers to the following two questions before going further:

    — How did closing yourself off from constructive criticism affect your relationship to the other person?

    — What was the effect of your response on your own self-esteem?

When you discount the suggestions or input of others, even if their comments aren't valid, you damage your relationship with them. Jesus discussed the subject of criticism, forgiveness, and mutually acceptable compromises in a passage quoted earlier: "Therefore, if you are offering your gift at the altar and there remember that your brother has something against you, leave your gift there in front of the altar. First go and be reconciled to your brother; then come and offer your gift" (Matthew 5:23-24).

Jesus said that if we are aware that someone has a criticism of us, we should go, give that person an opportunity to express his or her criticism, and attempt to respond in a way that encourages reconciliation. Our earthly relationships are to be set straight before we attempt to worship the Lord. Here are five steps for dealing positively with criticism.

• Ask for details. For example, if someone says, "You're too rigid!" you might respond by asking, "In what ways do you see me as being rigid?" It's easy to become defensive about general criticism because you always can point out specific instances where you're not that way. However, specific details may help you see the validity of the criticism.

• Summarize the criticism. Summarizing and restating the criticism allows two things to happen: It shows the other person that you have heard his input, and it helps you determine whether or not you have correctly understood the point.

• Agree with the criticism. This doesn't necessarily mean that you immediately agree that the criticism is correct. You might agree with the critic's right to an opinion even if you don't agree that the criticism has validity. On another level, you might agree with some parts of the criticism and disagree with other parts. Or you might agree that the criticism is primarily accurate and modify your own behavior in light of what has been said.

Agreeing with someone else's criticism at one of these levels usually has a disarming effect. When most people criticize someone, they expect that person to become defensive. When you listen to their criticism, summarize it to make sure that you've heard it correctly, and then indicate that you'll carefully consider their input, often much of their anger dissipates immediately. Even if you eventually end up concluding that you don't agree with them, the fact that you've carefully considered what they said often allows the relationship to continue in a strong and healthy manner.

• Explain your point of view. This can be helpful, whether or not you eventually change your own behavior. If you choose not to change your behavior, your explanation may help the other person understand your decision. By understanding your reasoning, the other person may find he or she is no longer bothered by your behavior. If you do change your behavior as a result of the criticism, your explanation may reduce any hurt or anger that they might have had because of your behavior. Understanding each other's perspective often brings healing in relationships.

• Work out a mutually acceptable change in behavior. If you agree or partially agree with the criticism and decide that a change in behavior is warranted, attempt to find a solution that will consider the needs and feelings of both persons. If both people don't feel counted in the solution, it won't be a totally satisfactory resolution. (Chapter 9 will give you more information about developing mutually acceptable resolutions.)

Mark Hammond, a fifty-five-year-old carpenter, has always prided himself in his ability to drive safely. But he recently started taking medication that causes drowsiness, and his wife Clara claims that he shouldn't be driving anymore. Her insinuation that he can't drive safely makes him very angry, and he responds with passive-aggressive comments about *her* driving habits. They have a heated argument followed by several days of silence. Everyone around them recognizes the rift. Let's look at how this situation could have been handled differently.

Clara: "I don't think you should be driving while you're on that medication."

Mark: "What is it about my driving that makes you think it isn't safe?" (asks for details).

Clara: "Well, you get very angry whenever something doesn't go your way, and I feel anxious that sometime your anger is going to cause you to do something dangerous" (describes the behavior, and expresses her feelings).

Mark: "So you're frightened because I'm not controlling my temper, afraid that this may cause me to do something impulsive that would be harmful?" (repeats and summarizes). "Is there anything else I do that makes you feel nervous with my driving?" (asks for details).

Clara: "Yes, there is one other thing. When traffic is heavy, you drive faster and closer to other cars than I feel comfortable with. If the person in front of you stops short, I'm afraid you wouldn't have time to stop without hitting the other car" (describes behavior and expresses feelings).

Mark: "So a second thing that makes you feel anxious when I drive is following too closely in heavy traffic?" (repeats criticism).

Clara: "Yes."

Mark: "I can see how those things might make you feel uncomfortable with my driving. While I don't think either is dangerous, I'm willing to change them if that would make you more comfortable" (agrees with her right to her perspective, shows willingness to modify behavior). "Driving is very important to me. To give that up would make me feel old and dependent, something I'm not ready for" (explains his point of view). "Would you feel comfortable with the following compromise? I'll try to control my temper at other drivers, and I'll try to leave more distance between myself and other cars, if you'll agree to quit telling me that I shouldn't be driving" (attempting to work out a mutually acceptable compromise).

Clara: "That sounds fine to me, but I want to clarify one thing: If you are following more closely than I feel comfortable with, I want to be able to tell you how I feel and have you leave a little more room without causing a major confrontation between us. Is that okay with you?" (redefines compromise so that both parties are satisfied with it).

Mark: "That's fine."

Refer to the situation you wrote about a few moments ago in your notebook. Write out a dialogue of how you might have responded more openly to the other person's criticism, using the five suggested steps for dealing with criticism. You may have to hypothesize what that person would have said if you had positively received their criticism. After doing this on paper, consider if it would be helpful to go back to that person and reopen that conversation. If we want people to be open to our assertiveness or criticism, we must be open to theirs as well.

Dealing with Negative Responses to Your Assertiveness
When someone rejects your initial assertive statement and attempts to detour you back into being nonassertive, you may be tempted to give up and return to your former patterns of behavior. However, as a Christian parent, spouse, employee, church member, or friend, you shouldn't allow yourself to be intimidated when a legitimate problem needs to be resolved.

Even if you've developed a perfect assertive script, a person with whom you have a conflict may react in totally unexpected ways. The other person may deny the validity of your statements, blame the problem on you or someone else, begin a long-winded self-defense, or shift the discussion to a completely unrelated trait of yours. All of these are obvious attempts to detour you, but you can learn how to get a conversation back on track.[2]

Attempts to detour fall into five main categories. The other person may try to:
- Avoid dealing with the issue.
- Deny the validity of your assertive statement.
- Collapse into a "poor me" stance so that you withdraw your criticism.
- Make excuses for the behavior.
- Strike back at you.

The remainder of this chapter will discuss various assertive techniques that can be used with the Triple-A Model to help you be assertive initially, or help you maintain an assertive stance when someone tries to detour you from it.

Twelve Assertive Techniques[3]
In the past twenty-five years a large number of assertive techniques have been developed. I believe that some of these writings and teachings have not taken adequate care to distinguish assertive techniques from countermanipulative techniques, that is, techniques designed to counter or oppose a manipulative person.

An assertive technique gives people the power to decide for themselves what they will think, feel and do in a way that shows respect for the thoughts and feelings of both persons in the relationship. It functions out of an "I count me, I count you" framework.

A countermanipulative technique helps a person avoid being manipulated by another. It is not concerned as much with showing respect for the thoughts and feelings of the other person as it is with enabling the user to not be manipulated. Thus, those who are on the receiving end of a countermanipulative technique may feel very frustrated, because it operates from an "I count me, I don't count you" perspective. An example of a countermanipulative technique is *fogging*. The person using the "fogging" technique responds like a cloud or a bank of fog: he or she absorbs whatever statements the manipulative person makes (sometimes even summarizing the person's complaint), but does not make any commitment to change his or her behavior. Thus the manipulator loses control over the other person. However, the "fogging" technique is so frustrating to the recipient that the relationship can be seriously damaged. If assertiveness means "speaking the truth in love," I don't believe "fogging" fits this definition. There are assertive ways to avoid being manipulated that are not so damaging to relationships.

The twelve assertive techniques listed below can become unloving (aggressive) if used rigidly and without care for the other person. However, if used with love and good judgment, they can give us the freedom to think, feel and behave as *we* choose, and not be intimidated or manipulated by others. They can be used carefully so that the other person feels respected and cared for. None of these techniques by itself can be used in every situation: however, if you know all of them you'll have the ability to be assertive and to maintain your assertiveness in almost any situation.

1. Broken record. This method gets its name because it sounds like a broken record: the same line, with few variations, is used over and over. This method is especially helpful when someone tries to manipulate you. For example:

Encyclopedia salesperson: "This special sale price is the lowest you'll ever hear, so I know that you don't want to pass up this opportunity."

You (politely but firmly): "We've decided not to invest in a home encyclopedia set right now" (initial assertive response).

Salesperson: "I understand that, but I know that you are the kind of parents who want your children to excel in school.

Right? And don't you agree that having these encyclopedias in your home would help them do better in school?" (manipulation).

You: "We've decided not to invest in a home encyclopedia set at this time" (broken record).

Salesperson: "Listen, I'll level with you. Our company is sponsoring a special promotion. If I sell only two more sets this week, I'll win a week's vacation in Hawaii. My wife sure is looking forward to it, and since you need these encyclopedias for your children's education, let's try to work out something" (manipulation).

You: "We've decided not to buy your encyclopedias right now" (broken record).

Salesperson: "I guess you're really determined not to buy this set from me."

You: "Right. You made a fine presentation, and I hope you win the trip" (Affirmation). "And if you will leave your business card with me, I'll be glad to pass your name on to any of my friends who want encyclopedias" (workable compromise).

Broken Record puts *you* in control of what you will and will not do. Manipulators know that they can wear most people down with three objections, but the Broken Record lets you stand by your decision, no matter how many objections they raise. Broken Record also allows you to remain calm and polite while staying firm, because you don't have to get flustered trying to think of an answer to each of the manipulator's statements.

Broken Record is an excellent technique to use when you know what you want to do, you aren't responsible for meeting the other person halfway, and you want to avoid being manipulated away from that position. It's a good way to get practice at refusing requests or demands and be able to experience the exhilaration that comes with being able to say no when you mean no.

There is a disadvantage to Broken Record. Since you never really answer the objections of the manipulative person, he or she may think that you aren't really listening, and that may cause frustration. If the person is a salesperson whom you will never see again, that disadvantage may be of little concern to you. But if you have an ongoing relationship, you may want to use a modification of the Broken Record described below.

2. Broken record plus. With this method you summarize the other person's points, then you return to your repeated phrase. This helps the person see that you are paying attention. Let's return to the encyclopedia salesperson and see how this interchange would sound using Broken Record Plus.

Salesperson: "This special sale price is the lowest that will ever be offered. Surely you don't want to pass up this excellent opportunity" (manipulation).

You: "That is a very good price, and you have a very good encyclopedia, but we've decided not to invest in a home encyclopedia set right now" (Broken Record Plus, agreeing with a valid point but maintaining the right to make one's own decision).

Salesperson: "I know that you're the kind of parents who want your children to excel in school. Right? And don't you agree that having these encyclopedias in your home would help them to do better in school?" (manipulation)

You: "Yes, we would like our children to do well in school, and it certainly would be convenient for them to have encyclopedias here at home. However, they do have easy access to encyclopedias at school and at our local public library, which is just down the street. For those reasons I don't believe we need to have an encyclopedia set in our home, and therefore I don't plan to invest in this set" (Broken Record Plus, agreeing with valid points but maintaining the right to make one's own decision).

Salesperson: "Let me level with you. Our company is sponsoring a special promotion. Two more sets sold and I can take my wife to Hawaii. You need a set of encyclopedias, you've already agreed that it's a good price, and you can help me win a trip at the same time. Now, wouldn't you like to go ahead and make a decision that would help all of us?" (manipulation)

You: "I do hope that you win the trip, and it is a very good price, but my decision is firm: We're not going to invest in a home encyclopedia set right now. If you will leave your business card with me, I'll be glad to pass your name on to any of my friends who may be interested in home encyclopedias now" (Broken Record Plus and workable compromise).

Broken Record Plus requires more thinking on your feet than Broken Record, but it alleviates some of the other person's frustration at thinking that you're not listening. The other person still may be frustrated that you didn't give in to their manipulation, but he or she doesn't have the added frustration of believing that you weren't listening. Broken Record Plus is an excellent counter reply when you are certain that the other person is being manipulative, has some valid points, but has a goal that is different from yours.

3. Sorting issues. Whenever people receive criticism and decide to become defensive rather than be open to it, they may decide to strike back with a criticism that is unrelated to your original issue. A common result is that the conversation (or argument) moves to *their* topic instead of yours, and your issue is ignored and unresolved. If you sort the issues, you differentiate your issue from theirs, assertively directing the discussion back to the topic you brought up. As you do so, you can agree to discuss their issue at a later time.

4. Disagreeing. One of the most simple assertive counter-replies is to make a straightforward, direct statement—"I don't agree with. . . ."

5. Emphasizing thoughts/feelings. Another assertive technique to ward off detours is to emphasize (or reemphasize) the importance of your thoughts or feelings about the behavior or situation ("This is very important to me.") One way to do this is to give more details in the Assertion part of your statement. Another is to emphasize the importance to you of resolving the issue. Let's look at an example of how this could work.

Mother: "I appreciated your attitude last week when we discussed sharing the family workload so that I could continue to work and help pay the expense of your college tuition. Our agreement will mean more work for you and your brother, but I hope it will enable your father and I to continue to help you with college costs" (affirmation).

"Part of the agreement was that you would do the family wash on Tuesdays and Saturdays. I'm disappointed that you didn't do your part the very first week of our agreement" (assertion).

Daughter: "C'mon Mom, lighten up! It's only Wednesday. Why do you have to get so upset about the wash not being done one day?" (attempt to detour)

Mother: "I'm upset because you agreed to share the house-work and because you didn't follow through on your part of the agreement" (emphasize thoughts/feelings).

Daughter: "You're right. I'll try to do it tonight or tomor-row. I'm supposed to meet Judi at the mall in 30 minutes, but I promise to do it later" (attempt to detour).

Mother: "Tonight you have practice with the youth choir. You're going to have difficulty going to the mall, practicing with the youth choir, doing your homework, *and* doing the wash—all tonight. That's why we decided on Tuesdays and Saturdays. But that's not the primary issue here." (Sorting issues) "The thing that frustrates me is that you made an agreement and on the very first day didn't keep your end of the bargain" (emphasize thoughts/feelings).

Daughter: "You're right, but why are you coming down so hard on me? I've got a lot to do, especially compared to my friends" (another attempt to detour).

Mother: "I'm not talking to you about how much you have to do compared with what your friends have to do" (Sorting issues). "What I'm talking to you about here is my frustration that you didn't follow through on a commitment you made, *the very first time* that commitment came up" (emphasize thoughts/ feelings).

Daughter: "Okay. Okay. I'll call it off with Judi and do it right now."

6. Redefining. Sometimes a person will attempt to detour your attempts to be assertive by defining your behavior or attitude in negative terms; for example, "You're just too picky," or "You're being too sensitive." Your best counter-reply may be to redefine your behavior in positive ways: "I don't think I'm being too picky; I'm concerned because I want us to have a good relationship. And I think if this problem continues without being resolved, it will definitely damage our marriage" (or friendship).

7. Answering quickly. When the other person attempts to detour you by asking a question that requires many details or long discussion, it's important to assess his request and moti-

vation. If the request is for legitimate information that is related to the issue, it may be worthwhile to allow the conversation to digress temporarily, as long as you eventually bring the conversation back to your issue.

On the other hand, if you recognize the request for extensive information as an attempt to detour you from the primary issue, it's best to give a brief answer, either yes or no or a direct reply, and then immediately bring the discussion back to the primary issue.

8. Negative inquiry. Sometimes people will attempt to manipulate us or deflect an assertive request away from themselves by making a vague criticism of us; "You're too bossy" or "You're inconsiderate." Instead of accepting vague criticisms, it's important to ask for clarification: "In what ways do you think I'm too bossy?" or "Would you give me some examples where I've been inconsiderate?"

Negative inquiry (inquiring about the negative) can be a helpful assertive technique in at least two ways. First, if people are attempting to manipulate us by making a vague criticism, this will become evident by their inability to come up with specifics. Secondly, if it is a valid and genuine criticism, more concreteness will enable us to change our behavior appropriately.

9. Negative assertion. Sometimes people will attempt to detour us by making a criticism that is valid, then adding to it another criticism that we believe is invalid, or drawing a conclusion that doesn't necessarily follow from the part of their criticism that is valid.

If we disagree with both points they are making, the valid one and the invalid one, we end up becoming defensive about the part of their criticism that is valid. A more healthy response is to use negative assertion: agree with the part of their criticism that is valid (assert the negative), but then disagree with the part of the assertion or the conclusion that you think is invalid.

John and his neighbor Frank had a casual friendship. John is a Christian; Frank is a confirmed skeptic about religion and religious people. In an evening conversation on John's patio, Frank launched into a tirade about television evangelists who had abused donations that had been sent to them and implied that all television ministries were scams (valid criticism of one situation, invalid conclusion).

Using Negative Assertion, John agreed with some of the specific abuses that Frank had pointed out, and agreed with the need for greater accountability for those who solicit donations. However, John then went on to document several television ministries that were doing a great deal of good with money they had collected, and he argued that many people involved in such ministries were sincere and were helping those who would otherwise not be helped (agreed with accurate part of the criticism, disagreed with the invalid conclusion).

10. Repeating the action line. If you believe you are making a legitimate assertive request and the other person is trying to manipulate you, you may decide that the best way to deal with this is to stand firm by repeating your action line until it is heard.

For example, a group of employees in a Christian organization all felt the same way about a certain behavior of one of their work supervisors, so they sent her a joint letter explaining their concern and indicating their desire to talk with her about this as a group. She responded that she wanted to talk with them individually. It was their belief that she wanted to do this in order to individually blame one of the group for the criticism directed at her and to intimidate the rest of the group into withdrawing their criticism.

The group decided to maintain their original action line: she would have to discuss the issue with the group, since it was legitimately a group issue and not just one person's complaint. They would not meet with her if she scheduled individual sessions with them. She reluctantly agreed to meet with them together to discuss the issue.

11. Developing a workable compromise. Sometimes after presenting your point of view and hearing the other person's response, you may realize that there would be value in meeting the other person somewhere in the middle (that is, modifying your original action line). Willingness to negotiate is crucial in any healthy relationship, and certainly is part of biblical assertiveness (Philippians 2:4). It's important to distinguish between appeasement—giving in because of fear or

intimidation—and workable compromise—awareness of your goals, understanding the other person's goals, and attempting to construct a positive solution that respects both person's goals.

12. Stipulating consequences. Usually it is sufficient to use a three-part assertive statement and reinforce that with the eleven assertive techniques mentioned above. But in occasional situations the other person may use so many detours or maintain such a nonnegotiating stance that these assertive techniques will not be sufficient.

When pushed to the limits of tolerance by the other person's detours, there are times when you may decide to consider a promise of realistic, negative consequences if the offensive behavior continues. Since stipulating negative consequences may be viewed by the other person as a threat or ultimatum, this approach should be used only when necessary.

Social consequences may be highly motivating, particularly when people are social equals and both want to maintain a good relationship. Positive social consequences could include: "If you will do that, I'd appreciate it a lot." Or, "If you do that, I think it will make our friendship stronger." Negative social consequences might be: "If you continue that behavior even though you know it hurts me, it will damage our relationship."

If you expect that you may have to stipulate negative consequences in order to motivate the other person to consider your request, think through possible consequences ahead of time. A consequence that is made while the conversation is deteriorating is not likely to be as good as one to which you have given forethought. Make sure that you are willing to carry out the consequence if the request or some reasonable compromise is not met. For a consequence to be effective, the other person must be convinced that you will act.

A negative consequence will generally have greater impact if it is logically related to the troubling behavior. For example, the parent of a chronically late teenager might say: "If you are in by curfew, you may date according to the terms we have discussed. If you are more than fifteen minutes past curfew, you lose dating privileges for one week."

The seriousness of the stipulated consequences should be proportional to the seriousness of the offense. In general it is best to begin by presenting the mildest consequence that you think will be effective in motivating the other person to change. This is sometimes referred to as using the "minimally effective response." Then escalate the severity of the threatened consequence only if necessary.

For example, Kathy started experiencing some sexual harrassment from her male boss. Initially she responded with mild assertive responses such as "Don't do that!" or "I don't think that's funny!" The unwelcome behavior continued, so Kathy realized she needed to escalate her assertion by stipulating some negative consequences. This is what she wrote to her boss, dating the letter and keeping a copy for her own records:

> I know that you are aware that it is illegal to sexually harrass your employees. I have asked you four times to stop, but you have continued to bother me. I want you to know that I have begun compiling a list of your actions that are sexually harrassing, along with the dates on which you did these things. If you persist in this behavior, I will continue to add to the list and at some point turn it over to the proper authorities. If you discontinue this behavior, I will be able to work more effectively for you and will eventually destroy the list.

KEY IDEAS FROM CHAPTER 8

1. If you want others to be open to your assertive requests for changes in *their* behavior, you should make sure that you are equally open to their request for changes in *your* behavior.

2. If you have been nonassertive for many years and suddenly begin to be assertive, you should expect that at least some people will attempt to detour you back into your nonassertive ways.

3. Attempts to detour fall into five main categories. A person may try to
   • Avoid dealing with the issue.

- Deny the validity of the assertive statement.
- Collapse into a "poor me" stance so that you withdraw the criticism.
- Make excuses for the behavior.
- Strike back at the assertive person.

4. In addition to the Triple-A Model of Assertiveness, there are twelve assertive techniques that can be used when people try to detour you back into nonassertiveness. These are:

- Broken Record
- Broken Record Plus
- Sorting Issues
- Disagreeing
- Emphasizing Thoughts/Feelings
- Redefining
- Answering Quickly
- Negative Inquiry
- Negative Assertion
- Repeating the Action Line
- Developing a Workable Compromise
- Stipulating the Consequences

EXERCISES

This chapter on detours has a great deal of important content in it. I would recommend that you do exercises 1 through 4 this week, read the chapter again and do the remainder of the exercises next week.

Write in your notebook your answers to the following questions:

1. In your own words write out a definition of each of the twelve assertive techniques. Also identify what kind of situation this technique might be best suited for. If you can't remember either of the above, reread that section of this chapter and write out the definitions and descriptions in your own words.

2. Do you think any of the twelve assertive techniques discussed in this chapter are incompatible with Scripture? If so, which ones? What makes you believe they are incompatible?

3. Which of these twelve techniques would be most difficult for you to use? What would make it difficult for you to use those particular methods?

4. Identify two situations where you have been detoured from being assertive. For each of those situations:
• Describe what happened.
• Identify one or more assertive techniques you could have used against that detour.
• Write out an assertive reply using that/those technique(s).

5. Identify the five classes of detours listed in this chapter, describing them in your own words. The description need not be lengthy—one or two lines is sufficient.

6. List the kinds of detours used most frequently by the people around you. (These detours can be ones used against you personally or ones you observe being used against others.)

7. What kinds of detours do you find most difficult to deal with? What do you think makes it particularly difficult to deal with that kind of detour? (If you have no one who tries to detour you, think about which of these detours would probably be most difficult for you to deal with if they were used on you. Why would those be particularly difficult for you?)

8. From your Personal Assertiveness Inventory (chapter 2), pick out two situations in which you have difficulty being assertive. Write up an initial Triple-A Model script, then write down ways that people might try to detour you. Lastly, write out assertive replies that you could use to respond to those detours. Write down what you would say as well as the skill or type of detour that is being used.

NINE

The Art of Negotiation

Make my joy complete by being like-minded, having the same love, being one in spirit and purpose. Do nothing out of selfish ambition or vain conceit, but in humility consider others better than yourselves. Each of you should look not only to your own interests, but also to the interests of others.

—Philippians 2:2-4

Most of us approach conflict with a win/lose mentality. Either you win and I lose, or I win and you lose. With this approach, one person usually escalates his or her assertiveness (or aggressiveness) until the other person gives in. Some people are so uncomfortable with conflict or afraid of it that their partners easily and regularly "win."

However, there are several reasons why such "winning" is not really winning. If the "losing" person regularly feels uncounted in the relationship, he or she is likely to have progressively lower self-esteem, more depression, more physical illnesses, and less enthusiasm for the relationship. The "winner" may miss valuable ideas and insights that could be gained by listening to the other person. The "winner" is also providing a poor example of what Christian love and the Christian life are all about. The "loser" may eventually get enraged by this kind of aggression and leave the relationship.

When our energies are invested in winning, we may miss possibilities for workable compromises because we don't listen carefully to other's goals, and we aren't looking for compromises that would meet their goals and ours.

Relationship Credo
The following Relationship Credo suggests an alternative to the win/lose pattern of resolving differences:

You and I are in a relationship which I value and want to keep . . . yet each of us is a separate person with his own unique needs and the right to try to meet those needs. I will try to be genuinely accepting of your behavior, both when you are trying to meet your needs and when you are having trouble meeting your needs.

When you share your problems, I will try to listen acceptingly and understandingly in a way that will facilitate your finding your own solutions rather than depending upon mine. When you have a problem because my behavior interferes with your meeting your needs, I encourage you to tell me openly and honestly how you feel. At those times I will listen and then try to modify my behavior.

However, when your behavior interferes with my meeting my own needs, thus causing me to feel unaccepting of you, I will tell you as openly and honestly as I can exactly how I am feeling, trusting that you respect my needs enough to listen and then try to modify your behavior.

At those times when neither of us can modify our behavior to meet the needs of the other, thus finding that we have a conflict of needs in our relationship, let us commit ourselves to resolve each such conflict without ever resorting to the use of either my power or yours to win at the expense of the other losing. I respect your needs, but I also must respect my own. Consequently, let us strive always to search for solutions to our inevitable conflicts that will be acceptable to both of us. In this way your needs will be met, but so will mine. No one will lose; both will win.

As a result you can continue to develop as a person through meeting your needs and so can I. Our relationship can always be a healthy one because it will be mutually satisfying. Thus each of us can become what he is capable of being, and we can continue to relate to each other in mutual respect, friendship, love, and peace. Author unknown

The Relationship Credo suggests that when we have a differ-

ence with someone else, we consciously choose to drop the win/lose approach. Instead we should
- listen carefully so we understand our partner's goals,
- tune into our own self-awareness so that we can be clear about our own thoughts, feelings, and intentions,
- see if together we can come up with some creative alternative that satisfies both persons' goals.

The mind-set of negotiation takes into account both persons' goals. It keeps us from entering a discussion as if the other person were an opponent. The other party, instead, becomes a collaborator and partner who is also trying to develop a mutually satisfying solution.

Workable Compromises
Your openness to consider workable compromises in a given situation depends on several factors. If you believe you have a reasonable request and that your partner is only trying to manipulate you back onto a passive position, you may decide that you are going to stand firm on your "Action" line and refuse to be manipulated or persuaded to change your mind.

On the other hand, after hearing the other person's point of view you may acknowledge that he or she also has some valid points and reasonable goals. If you remain uncompromising about the change you specify, your partner may view you as selfish and insensitive. In these situations it's best to work toward a workable compromise, because then both people feel counted in the solution.

A compromise might take any of the following forms:[1]
- Find a mutually satisfying alternative. As in all negotiating, it's important to find out what goals are important to each person. After sharing your goals with each other and finding that you have conflicting intentions, you might want to create a new solution to the problem that takes into account both persons' needs or wants. This new solution may be different than the goal either of you initially proposed.

For example, Hal and Marie attended a church that sponsored fellowship groups one Saturday evening each month. Both Hal and Marie enjoyed going to these meetings, but a difference of opinion about whether to continue to be involved in the groups eventually developed. Marie, who worked at home taking care of their two preschoolers, loved these get-togethers as an opportunity to have a break from the children and enjoy some adult stimulation. Hal, who had to work Saturdays until just before the fellowship started, preferred to spend Saturday evening at home with his wife and children. In their initial discussion Hal and Marie identified the individual needs each felt. It seemed like a win/lose situation: either they went to the fellowship groups (Marie wins, Hal loses) or they stayed home (Hal wins, Marie loses).

One possible compromise seemed to be for Marie to go by herself. That was workable, but not very satisfying. Marie disliked attending the couple-oriented fellowship by herself, and Hal didn't enjoy those Saturday evenings at home without Marie. Then they used their creativity to come up with a better solution: Hal arranged to get off work early on the one Saturday each month when the fellowship group was scheduled. He then could spend a few hours with his children before he left with Marie for the fellowship meeting.

Hal and Marie wouldn't have arrived at the best compromise if they had remained locked in a win/lose mentality. The mutually satisfying alternative, which is often the best kind of workable compromise, appeared only when they began looking for a new solution that was different from the one either one of them had initially proposed.

Acts 6 records a well-known biblical incident that uses this kind of compromise. The Grecian Jews complained to the apostles because they believed their widows were being neglected in the daily distribution of food (v. 1). The apostles listened to the complaint and apparently considered it for a time before replying. The goal of the Grecian Jews was to ensure that their widows were properly cared for: the apostles' goal was not to be distracted from their most important priority—ministering the Word of God (v. 2). Therefore the apostles proposed a mutually satisfying alternative: they appointed deacons who would see that the widows' needs were not neglected and at the same time allow the apostles to continue their pastoral ministry unencumbered (vv. 3-7). It's interesting that even though the Grecian Jews approached the problem in a passive-aggressive manner (complaining), the apostles responded in an assertive manner (looking for an

"I count you, I count me" solution), and the matter was resolved successfully.

• Develop a quid pro quo contract. The Latin term *quid pro quo* means "this for that." In this type of compromise, one person agrees to change something in exchange for a change on the part of the other person.

As an example, John was frustrated that his fourteen-year-old son, Jack, never seemed to listen to him. John talked repeatedly with his son, but got no results. Finally Jack told his father that the reason he "tuned him out" was because John never said anything positive to him: "You're always putting me down and complaining about my behavior."

John was taken aback by this, but after thinking about it, he realized that Jack was correct. John offered the following quid pro quo compromise, which Jack agreed to: John would make an effort to look for things that Jack was doing well, rather than focusing on mistakes. He would try to give more compliments and fewer criticisms. In turn, Jack would make an effort to listen carefully when his father spoke to him.

• Take turns. If a source of conflict is repeated, two people can agree to take turns meeting their respective goals. Joe and Fran had disagreements for years over vacations. He loved the ruggedness of camping out in the mountains, but she enjoyed the more comfortable setting of a nice hotel suite beside the beach. As they grew older, their children were torn between their parents' preferences.

Eventually Joe and Fran compromised by taking turns. One vacation would be in the mountains, the next would be at the beach. Once the solution took effect and Joe and Fran no longer had to defend their respective positions, they were surprised to discover that they both enjoyed the other's preference nearly as much as their own.

• Separate solutions. Sometimes two people compromise by agreeing to separate temporarily to accomplish individual goals. In many families there seems to be an unwritten rule that husband and wife have to attend social events together. When children come, they are automatically added under this "umbrella" concept. Some families still operate under this unwritten rule for various reasons: "We always did it that way in my family." "We don't want people wondering if we're having family problems." "We just feel uncomfortable going places separately."

But if a husband likes hamburgers and country music, while his wife enjoys caviar and operas, there's nothing wrong with one sometimes going out alone or with a friend of similar tastes. The unwillingness to let the other spouse do some things separately in order to fulfill his or her needs may be a sign of unhealthy dependency, which comes when someone consciously or unconsciously believes that a particular person's presence is necessary for his or her happiness.

As mentioned in an earlier chapter, healthy people have a need for both contact and withdrawal in close relationships. If one person, because of unhealthy dependency, will not allow the other person to have any withdrawal time, the partner may begin to feel emotionally suffocated or trapped. Naturally, it's good for separation to be the exception rather than the norm in a marriage relationship. However, freedom to separate occasionally not only allows for more avenues of workable compromise, but it also may encourage a healthy independence in a relationship that has become overly dependent.

• Allow an involved third party to help make the decision. If two people's goals seem equally important and if other compromises aren't easily made, another party who is involved in the issue may be helpful in breaking the deadlock.

Monica and Matt, for instance, were having difficulty deciding whether to register their twelve-year-old daughter in a Christian school again, as they had for the past three years. Their daughter, Kimberly, loved the school, and they believed that the principles she was learning there made this the best alternative. The problem involved finances. Matt believed they could not afford the increased tuition. Monica understood the monetary problems but pushed for budget cuts—by taking no vacation trip and keeping their present car for another year.

Since the decision significantly involved Kimberly, Matt and Monica decided to include her input in making the final decision. They were careful to avoid "triangulating" their daughter (forcing her to decide between one or the other's position). Instead, they explained the pros and cons of each choice and indicated that they would like her input in the decision-making process since the decision would affect her life in several ways. Kimberly declared her desire to continue attending the Christian school, even if that meant staying home for vacation. That additional source of information helped make the resultant decision more satisfying for all.

Positive Yielding

Sometimes none of these five types of workable compromise results in a solution. When this occurs, positive yielding may be the answer. Positive yielding means deferring to the wants of the other person out of love, consideration, or respect. It is different from passivity in four significant ways.

● A passive person doesn't clearly identify his or her own goals or desires. With positive yielding, a person identifies his or her goal, discovers the other person's goals, searches for a workable compromise, but can find none. It is then that the person defers to the other person out of love.

● With passivity, the yielder doesn't count self, and thus decreases his or her own self-esteem. With positive yielding the person does count self, but voluntarily chooses to count the other person's desire higher than his or her own.

● With passivity, yielding is often done from a position of weakness as a result of fear or intimidation. In positive yielding, a person yields from a position of strength and choice.

● With passivity one person almost always gives in while the other person almost always gets his way. With positive yielding, each person yields in somewhat equal amounts.

Positive yielding is based on several Scriptures. Ephesians 5:21 speaks of submitting to one another out of reverence for Christ. Romans 12:10 and Philippians 2:3 both speak of honoring one another above one's own self. Jesus said it is more blessed to give than to receive. On the night He instituted the Lord's Supper, Jesus served His disciples and told them that as His followers, they should do likewise (John 13:5-17).

Negotiation Tips

● The negotiation process starts with your Triple-A script. As exchanges take place, summarize each other's messages before going on. This promotes careful listening and ensures that you understand the other's thoughts and feelings.

● If at any time either of you sense that you are losing control (in danger of becoming aggressive, passive-aggressive, or manipulative), ask for a "time out" and agree to continue at a later time, whether a few minutes or a few days.

● After a series of exchanges, go back and clarify your "action" line. If it has changed as a result of the discussion, a clarification will help define what you want your partner to do.

● Give the other person a chance to agree to your request or to propose an alternate resolution.

● If you can't agree on an acceptable change of behavior, clearly state the goal you would like to accomplish through your "action" line and ask your partner to identify his or her underlying goal.

● Use one of the five types of workable compromise to try to resolve your differences.

● If you can't come to a satisfactory agreement, arrange to come back at a specified time to work on the issue again.

● Throughout this whole process, pray for help in defining a workable compromise that will be satisfactory to both of you. If you can't find a satisfactory workable compromise, consider positive yielding.

● After settling on an acceptable resolution, follow through with each other, making sure that the compromise continues to be mutually satisfactory.

SUMMARY OF ASSERTIVENESS STEPS

At this point we have examined all the assertiveness steps developed in chapters 5 through 9. They are:

1. Stop the angry impulse before it comes out.

2. Identify the goal that has been blocked.

3. Decide whether the blocked goal is reasonable and is important enough to talk about.

4. If you decide that your goal is a legitimate and important one, communicate your goal to the other person. (The dimensions of awareness and the Triple-A Model of Assertiveness may be helpful here.)

5. Depending on who you are talking to, prepare yourself

for possible detours the person may use, and decide how you would respond to those detours.

6. Find out the other person's goal.

7. See if you can find a workable compromise. Workable compromises include:

● Finding a mutually satisfying alternative.

● Developing a quid pro quo contract.

● Taking turns.

● Temporarily separating.

● Allowing an involved third party to help make the decision.

8. If you can't find a mutually acceptable workable compromise, consider positive yielding.

EXERCISES

1. Read the following verses. What does each say about the win/lose mind-set?

● Proverbs 17:1

● Matthew 5:9 (Note: In the Hebrew culture, to be called the *son* of someone who was not your biological father emphasized the fact that you had some personal quality in common with that designated person.)

● Ephesians 5:21

● James 3:17-18

● 1 Peter 3:1-9

2. If you have been accustomed to arguing about differences (of opinions, goals, etc.) from a win/lose orientation, identify some thoughts that would make it difficult to shift to a workable compromise (win/win) orientation. What advantages would there be in making this change?

3. Many Christians have interpreted Ephesians 5:22-24, Colossians 3:18 and 1 Corinthians 11:3 to mean that wives should always yield to their husbands whenever there is a difference of opinion or goal. Do you agree with this? Why?

4. Describe two situations in which you think workable compromises might be worth trying. Which type of workable compromise would you propose?

TEN

Reinforcing Your Message with Nonverbal Behavior

All orators give two speeches at the same time: one that is heard, and one that is seen.

— *William Shakespeare*

Up to this point we have focused on becoming assertive in our verbal behavior. But there are several important reasons why we also must learn to become assertive in our nonverbal behavior. (Nonverbal behavior includes our tone of voice, the pitch and fullness of our voice, our facial expressions, the movements of our hands, arms, feet, and body, our closeness to distance from the other person, and so forth.)

Many research studies emphasize the importance of nonverbal components of assertive behavior.[1] If there is a discrepancy between our verbal and nonverbal communication, people will believe our nonverbal behavior more than our words.

For example, if you are visiting at a friend's house and notice that she keeps glancing at her watch every few minutes, you are likely to interpret this to mean that you are keeping her from some scheduled event that she doesn't want to miss. You may ask her if you are keeping her from something. If she says no yet continues to sneak furtive glances at the clock, you are likely to assume that she really wants to be somewhere else but that she's too nonassertive to tell you the truth. You assume that her nonverbal behavior is a more accurate indicator of her true feelings than are her words.

Let's apply this to assertiveness. If you have written a tactfully assertive statement and deliver this with accompanying assertive nonverbal behavior, you are likely to give the message that this is an important issue and that you expect serious consideration. If, on the other hand, you deliver an assertive script in a weak, timid manner, your nonverbal behavior says that you are feeling insecure, that you easily could be intimidated or detoured back into a nonassertive position. Therefore, if you want your verbal assertiveness to have maximum effectiveness, you must develop corresponding nonverbal assertive behaviors.

It is important to learn assertive nonverbal behavior because at least part of your self-concept comes from how you perceive yourself from moment to moment. For example, if you look at yourself in the mirror and perceive yourself as ugly, your self-concept is generally lowered; if you perceive yourself as looking good, your self-concept generally will be heightened.

As you interact with others, you are constantly involved in unconscious self-monitoring. Does your voice sound strong or weak, full or insecure? Do your hand gestures seem weak, ineffectual, inhibited? Or are they appropriate enhancements of your verbal message?

If you perceive your nonverbal behavior to be weak or nonassertive even though your words are assertive, your self-perceptions may cause you to become less and less self-confident. On the other hand, if you hear yourself speaking in a normal, full voice, and acting with appropriately assertive hand and body gestures, your self-confidence is likely to increase, even if you initially were anxious about being assertive. As William James said: "To feel brave, act as if you were brave ... and a courage fit will very likely replace the fit of fear."

Let's look at some of the kinds of nonverbal behavior that can either enhance or undermine verbal assertiveness.

Gestures
Gestures can either enhance or detract from assertive communication. Some hand and arm movements may detract from the effectiveness of your message:

- A complete lack of hand and arm movements often is

interpreted by an audience as indicating timidity, fear, or rigidity.

• Overly enthusiastic gestures may be interpreted as attempts to be showy or to cover our anxiety.

• Abrupt or incomplete gestures often are interpreted as an indication of tension.

• Covering one's mouth while talking is often interpreted as lack of self-confidence.

• Distracting gestures such as scratching one's head, tinkering with jewelry, or adjusting one's clothing are likely to be interpreted as indications that a person is ill-at-ease. These movements definitely distract listeners from our verbal message.

Tom is a twenty-five-year-old whose nonverbal behavior at the beginning of counseling led one to believe that he was timid, afraid, uneasy, and tense. Tom was raised by a very nonexpressive and nonaffirming father, from whom he never received the validation that could have helped him feel okay about himself. Tom's mother was constantly critical of him, although she viewed her criticism as a way of helping him become all he could become. As a result of nonaffirmation from his father and constant criticism from his mother, Tom was filled with fear that he would not measure up but would fail in everything that he did. His nonverbal behavior conveyed this message: although he was a well-proportioned six-footer, Tom walked and gestured like a timid church mouse. As he talked, he either used no hand and arm movements at all or his movements were so weak that they were dwarfed by his physical size. The contrast between his larger than average physical size and his absent or miniscule physical gestures gave the message to the world that he felt very insecure.

Two kinds of gestures will enhance the effectiveness of any assertive and confident communication. *Descriptive gestures* "paint a picture in the sky" and include any kind of arm, hand, or body movements that enhance your verbal descriptions. *Emphatic gestures* emphasize a certain point. Emphatic gestures can be either positive (e.g. encircling someone with your arms as you say "I really love you") or negative (using more intense eye contact and a firmer voice as you say, "This is important to me, and I'm frustrated that you're treating it as if it were a joke!'").

If you find that you haven't been using hand and arm gestures in your speaking, you can take several simple steps to begin using them. First, give yourself permission to experiment with descriptive and emphatic gestures. Second, observe other people who use gestures particularly effectively or ineffectively. Become aware of the difference in impact those people have on you. Third, experiment with changes in your own hand and arm gesturing. You probably will not feel comfortable with major changes all at once, and large changes will seem unnatural to those who know you well. Therefore start with small increases in hand and arm gesturing, and then make further ones as you feel comfortable.

Posture and Body Tension
Changing posture can change the way we feel about ourselves and the impact we have on other people. Although we may not be conscious of it, we stoop when we maintain too little muscle tension. Others are likely to interpret this as tiredness, a lack of self-confidence, a feeling of discouragement or lack of self-worth. On the other hand, too much body tension may be interpreted as rigidity, an air of superiority, or fear.

A person who leans back during a conversation may be viewed as being disinterested, unfriendly, or attempting to cover up feelings of insecurity by maintaining a distance. When we cross our arms, we're suggesting that we're placing a barrier between ourselves and the other person. The same is true when we tightly close our legs or cross them so they point away from the other person.

In contrast to the above nonassertive postures, an assertive stance involves holding one's body and head comfortably erect, leaning slightly forward, with one's weight evenly distributed on both feet. Observe a confident speaker and you'll probably note each of these characteristics.

Distance
Proximity to other people also plays a direct role in the way people react to us. For a friend, a comfortable conversational

space allows approximately eighteen to thirty-six inches from face to face. With a stranger, the comfortable conversational space is three to five feet. When we are angry, we want more personal space, but as warmth between two people increases, we need less. Cultural customs also make a difference. People from Europe, the Middle East, and Latin America generally need a smaller personal space than North Americans and Asians do.

The kind of assertiveness this book tries to develop does not advocate the use of power tactics in order to be assertive. Rather, it involves an awareness of what behaviors give us more power when they are combined with positive efforts on our part to maintain or restore relationships.

If we are trying to defend our rights against an aggressive person, for example, we should maintain at least four feet between us and a stranger, and at least two feet between us and a friend. A distance less than this makes it hard for us to disagree assertively with the other person, whereas a distance more than this encourages fighting.

If we want to resolve the issue and yet avoid the use of power, we need to place ourselves on an equal level with others. We shouldn't stand when they are seated. We shouldn't sit on a higher or larger chair. We should sit next to them rather than across from them. If we do these things we obviously give up some power. However, issues that are resolved through use of power are often not resolved anyway, because the loser resents the winner's use of power to get their way.

Clothing and Grooming

Clothing and grooming affect how we feel about ourselves as well as how much respect others are likely to show us. Probably all of us have run down to the gas station or corner store in dirty clothes and with unwashed hair, hoping that no one who knows us will see us in such a condition. In contrast, we've probably all felt the confidence that comes from being well-dressed and knowing that we look our best. We are more likely to feel comfortable about being assertive when we feel good about the way we look.

If your clothes make you feel inferior or inadequate, consider giving them away, even if they are comfortable. This is particularly true if you are aware that these clothes decrease your self-confidence enough to inhibit healthy assertiveness.

The clothing you wear also influences the respect you receive from others. If you meet two strangers, one dressed in "grubbies" and the other dressed attractively, it's almost impossible not to feel a measurable difference in how much you initially respect and like the two. John Molloy, author of *Dress for Success,* puts it this way: "Successful dress cannot put a boob in the board room, but incorrect dress can definitely keep an intelligent, able man out."[2]

Cleanliness and moderate styles will generate more respect than will designer labels or strange fashions. Grooming should be done before a meeting, since touching hair, looking at fingernails, stroking a moustache, or adjusting clothing during a meeting can be interpreted as vanity or anxiety. The key word in grooming is balance. An assertive person reflects a healthy, clean appearance that is appropriate to the situation.

Voice Tone, Volume, and Pitch

One of the most valuable ways to express assertiveness is through vocal quality. Our tone of voice can be as important as the words we say. Tonal qualities can vary from gentle to harsh, from coldness to warmth.

An overly soft voice can communicate low self-confidence, passivity, or a tendency to be easily manipulated or intimidated. A voice that is too loud will normally be interpreted as indicating a demanding or aggressive personality. Ideally, the volume should fit the situation and should be varied to sustain interest. Also, most people will listen with more respect to a full-bodied voice than to one that is squeaky, harsh, or whiny.

The pitch of a person's voice also can help a person be assertive. A lower-pitched voice among both men and women is associated with strength, whereas a higher pitch suggests anxiety or insecurity. While natural sopranos and tenors will not speak in the same range as altos and basses, some people speak at a higher pitch than necessary. In such cases, practicing good breath support and consciously lowering the voice a few notes may produce a fuller and stronger voice.

In addition to fullness of voice and voice pitch, our inflection also affects how we are perceived. A wide range of speech tones generally commands greater interest and respect than a narrow inflective range. Professionally trained speakers such as Earl Nightingale and Paul Harvey often use an inflection range of at least sixteen musical notes. Their voices fluctuate as their subject matter, intensity, and intention change.

In summary, the most effective assertive voice is sufficiently loud to be heard comfortably, is full and resonant but not harsh and shrill, and has an interesting, moderate amount of vocal inflection.

Eye Contact and Expression

Passive people often look down or away from others when they speak. In some societies, it is considered disrespectful for women or younger people to make direct eye contact with men or older people. But in American society, lack of eye contact is seen as a sign of insecurity or timidity.

Aggressive or passive-aggressive people sometimes develop the habit of looking "past" or "through" others. It seems easier for aggressive people to disregard the needs or feelings of others if they do not tune into them with their eyes. At other times aggressive people may stare or glare at a conversational partner (watching rigidly or unblinkingly) or fix their gaze on an abnormality such as a bald spot or a birthmark. The unconscious intention here seems to be to intimidate the other person by making him or her feel self-conscious.

Specific qualities of eye contact and expression are consistent with an assertive style: Making direct eye contact and holding your head erect conveys a sincerity and an interest in what the other person is saying; blinking at a normal rate and "smiling" with relaxed eyes makes the other person feel accepted.

The muscles around our eyes can reflect a great deal of expressions—from strength to sadness, from hardness to hurt. Allowing your eyes to convey emotions appropriate to the specific verbal conversation helps enhance the verbal message that you have a healthy self-concept and that you genuinely care about the other person.

Facial Expressions

To increase the impact of assertiveness, our facial expressions must agree with our verbal comments. For example, if you desire to convey, "I'm genuinely interested in you," you should face the other person fully, maintain good eye contact, and lean just slightly toward the other person. A gentle smile is appropriate when first greeting someone: a flat or fearful expression will do little to convince other people that you are enjoying their conversation.

On the other hand, laughing or smiling while they are expressing anger or sadness will suggest that you don't take their feelings seriously. Laughing or smiling while you are expressing anger or sadness gives them a mixed message; they may be confused as to whether you are actually angry or sad or whether you are amused at the situation. Other facial mannerisms that distract from assertiveness include tensing or wrinkling your forehead, swallowing or clearing your throat excessively, and wetting your lips.

You probably will give inappropriate facial expressions if you allow your mind to wander as you listen to other people speak. If you begin thinking about a similar experience you've had or if you begin thinking about your response to what they're saying, your face will probably mirror what you're thinking about. If your facial expression doesn't match the content of their words, they'll probably conclude one of two things: that you don't have much empathy for their feelings or that you aren't listening to them. How do you keep from showing inappropriate facial expression when others are speaking? Tune in completely to them *until they have finished talking*. Don't allow your mind to wander to your own thoughts or to your response to them.

Remember that we communicate most effectively when our facial expressions and verbal messages match our intentions or goals. Sometimes we smile when we give constructive criticism or when we talk about something bothering us because we don't want other people to believe we're rejecting them. However, this approach presents a confusing message about how important the issue is to us.

If you remember to reassure the other person of your love and acceptance through the affirmation part of your assertive statement and if you have regularly encouraged the other person, then let your facial expressions be consistent with your true feelings when you discuss the behaviors you are asking them to change.

It's also valuable to know how people interpret nods. When we don't nod at all, most people assume that we disagree, are confused, or are disinterested. A single nod is often interpreted to mean that we agree. Occasional, slow nods are generally interpreted to mean that we understand what they are saying and are encouraging them to continue. Repeated and fast nods are usually understood as indications that we understand, agree, and want to interject our ideas into the conversation.

One well-known Christian speaker suggests that we should quit nodding whenever we no longer agree with what a person is saying. I disagree with this advice for several reasons. First, committed Christians have legitimate differences of opinion on some topics. If we stop nodding when people draw conclusions different from our own, our behavior may suggest that we'll accept them only when they agree with us.

Second, if we withdraw our nonverbal support by no longer nodding, the other person may stop talking and not tell us the entire situation. We may never get an opportunity to understand a behavior or idea in its total context.

Third, continuing to nod may help other people talk through the issue completely enough so that *they* may be able to hear their own unhealthy thinking and may be able to see the changes they need to make.

My own suggestion is to nod at appropriate times to let a person know that you hear what is being said and that you accept him or her as a person. If the person makes some assertions or comes to conclusions that you believe are seriously unbiblical or harmful (that is, they are not merely differences in preferences), you may want to discuss where you disagree and why. Nonverbal behavior can be easily misunderstood. If you quit nodding altogether, this might be interpreted as "I don't accept you" rather than "I disagree with some of your conclusions." By continuing to give an occasional nod as a person speaks, then disagreeing verbally with specific statements, you make it clear that you accept the person and are willing to hear him or her out fully, even though you may disagree.

Touch

Human touch is crucially important. Christ regularly reached out and physically touched not only His friends, but also strangers, even those considered untouchable because of their ailments.

Because of various fears, many Americans go through life rarely touching others or being touched. Yet many kinds of touch are healthy and appropriate—and available to us all. Most children would love to be touched and held more than they are. Many spouses would enjoy more touch than they presently receive. Shaking hands with those we meet deepens a sense of relationship more than a verbal greeting alone. A pat on the back, a hand on the shoulder or arm, or even a hug is often an appropriate gesture of warmth.

In his book *The Miracle of Touching,* Dr. John Hornbrook explores touching in American and other cultures. He concludes that children who are touched physically and emotionally by an adult authority figure are more considerate, altruistic, loving, and sharing. Frequency of touch is positively correlated with warmth, empathy, generosity, concern for others, and a positive self-image; people who touch others are more likely to be touched in return.[3]

As we noted in an earlier chapter, Virginia Satir, famed marriage and family therapist, believes, "We all need about eight hugs a day to feel healthy."

How is touch related to assertiveness? We can identify at least three ways: First, the assertive Christian is concerned about helping others become healthy persons. Appropriate touch can be an important way of increasing the emotional health of those around us.

Second, as we touch others, we are more likely to be touched in return. Healthy self-esteem is one of many things correlated with how frequently we are touched. And healthy self-esteem forms one of the bases for healthy assertiveness.

Third, research has shown that people who are assertive are not viewed as positively as people who are passive—unless the assertive communication includes extra affirmation.[4] Although assertiveness is not included in his study, Hornbrook's review of research makes it clear that people who touch are consistently viewed as warmer than those who do not. Therefore, there is an empirical basis for suggesting that appropriate touching can be one of the "extra affirmation" factors that makes assertiveness more positively regarded by those to whom we relate.

Pacing and Timing

Pacing refers to the rate at which we speak and the length of pauses we place between paragraphs. Speaking too rapidly may cause us to say things we'll regret and may cause others to view us as anxious or coercive. Speaking too slowly can cause others to view us as timid and unsure of ourselves. Speaking slowly for long periods of time may also cause others to become impatient with us.

Pausing too long between sentences can elicit two different kinds of interpretations. If other parts of our behavior betray insecurity, these pauses may be interpreted to mean that we're unsure of what we're going to say next. On the other hand, if we seem confident of what we're saying, people may become irritated with our long pauses. The pauses seem to be implying, "I've just said something very important, and I want you to have time to appreciate its significance before I go on."

The best pace for assertive communication is a moderate one, neither too rapid nor too slow.

Timing refers to choosing the best time to talk about issues of concern. Sometimes immediate expression of feelings is appropriate, especially in situations when hesitation would make later assertion less effective. For example, suppose a resolution has been made in a meeting and the vote is about to be taken. You have some reservations about the motion and haven't had time to clarify them in your own mind. You might say something like, "I have some reservations about the motion being considered, but I haven't had time to clarify those reservations. There may be others who also would like more time to think about the issue before voting. I suggest that we table the motion until next meeting to give us all time to think about it more thoroughly."

You can use a similar approach whenever someone is pushing you to make a decision without allowing you time to think through your thoughts on the matter.

Assertive timing should include three considerations: When will I feel prepared to discuss the issue? When will the other person feel prepared to discuss the issue? And, when are we likely to be free of distractions and disruptions?

KEY IDEAS FROM CHAPTER 10

1. A significant part of the impact of our communication comes from the nonverbal behavior that accompanies our words.

2. If there is a discrepancy between our words and our nonverbal behavior, people most often believe the nonverbal behavior.

3. If we are verbally assertive but our nonverbal behavior remains nonassertive, people are likely to believe that we could easily be intimidated or detoured back into a nonassertive stance.

4. For our verbal assertiveness to have maximum effectiveness, it must be accompanied by assertive nonverbal behavior.

5. Assertive nonverbal behavior includes:

● A moderate use of descriptive and emphatic gestures as we speak.

● Good posture and a moderate level of body tension.

● Maintaining an appropriate distance between ourselves and the other person.

● Moderate grooming and clothing styles.

● Speaking with a voice volume that allows us to be easily heard, keeping our voice full, and using moderate inflection.

● Maintaining steady eye contact with the person to whom we are speaking.

● Matching facial expressions to the content of the conversation.

• Using touch when appropriate.
• Speaking at a normal pace.
• Choosing the appropriate time to discuss important issues.

EXERCISES

1. Make three copies of the following checklist. Use one to rate yourself. Then give the others to two people who know you well and who will be honest with you. Tell the two people about this book and ask them to rate your nonverbal assertiveness as discussed in this chapter.

Gestures

Uses too few gestures	Yes ___ No ___
Gestures sometimes seem overly enthusiastic	Yes ___ No ___
Gestures sometimes seem abrupt or incomplete	Yes ___ No ___
Covers mouth when talking	Yes ___ No ___
Has distracting gestures	Yes ___ No ___

If yes, please explain: _____

_____

_____

Uses gestures that enhance verbal descriptions
Frequently ___ Sometimes ___ Rarely ___
Uses gestures that reinforce verbal emphases
Frequently ___ Sometimes ___ Rarely ___

Posture and Body Tension

Sometimes slouches or stoops	Yes ___ No ___
Has too much body tension	Yes ___ No ___
Leans away during conversations	Yes ___ No ___
Crosses arms or legs in ways that seem to put a barrier between self and other person	Yes ___ No ___

Distance

During friendly conversation, interpersonal distance seems
Too close ___ Too far away ___ About right ___

When standing up for rights, interpersonal distance seems
Too close ＿＿ Too far away ＿＿ About right ＿＿

Clothing and Grooming

Clothing usually clean and pressed   Yes ＿＿ No ＿＿
Dresses appropriately for the situation
Too dressed up ＿＿ Too casual ＿＿ About right ＿＿
Clothing style
Too unusual ＿＿ Too conservative ＿＿ About right ＿＿
Grooming complete before reaching
public situation   Yes ＿＿ No ＿＿

Voice Tone, Volume, and Pitch

Rate each category on a scale of 1 to 10.
Voice tone (1 means gentle and 10 means harsh) ＿＿＿＿＿
Voice warmth (1 means cold and 10 means warm) ＿＿＿＿
Fullness (1 means thin and 10 means full) ＿＿＿＿＿＿
Volume   Too soft ＿＿ Too loud ＿＿ About right ＿＿
Inflection Too little ＿＿ Too much ＿＿ About right ＿＿

Eye Contact and Expression

Maintains eye contact when listening or speaking
Most of the time ＿＿ Some of the time ＿＿ Rarely ＿＿
Appears to "look through" other person or glare or stare
Frequently ＿＿ Sometimes ＿＿ Rarely ＿＿
Eyes communicate rapport or empathy with the other person
Frequently ＿＿ Sometimes ＿＿ Rarely

Facial Expressions

When listening, person matches facial
expression to speaker's message   Yes ＿＿ No ＿＿
When speaking, person matches facial
expression to message
he or she is giving   Yes ＿＿ No ＿＿
Gives occasional nods when listening   Yes ＿＿ No ＿＿

Touch

Uses touch appropriately to enhance communication
Too much ＿＿ Too little ＿＿ About right ＿＿

Pacing and Timing

Rate of speech
    Too slow ____ Too fast ____ About right ____
Chooses an appropriate time to speak up
    Frequently ____ Sometimes ____ Rarely ____

2. Analyze your ability to make eye contact when talking or listening. Write your answers in your notebook.
   • How much of the time are you maintaining eye contact when speaking or listening?
   • Discuss with someone else your thoughts and feelings about eye contact. If you have self-talk that keeps you from feeling comfortable with eye contact, what can you say to dispute with that self-talk?
   • If you still find yourself uncomfortable making eye contact, practice focusing on a spot on the other person's forehead just between and slightly above his or her eyes. Gradually you will become more comfortable with eye contact.

3. Do you agree with the statement that you should continue nodding occasionally even when the speaker is saying something with which you disagree? Why or why not?

4. Analyze your ability to use touch appropriately in your relationships.
   • When and how do you use touch in your relationships? Do you think your family and close friends would benefit if you affirmed them more through touching?
   • If you are uncomfortable using touch at a level healthy for those around you, what "self-talk" produces this discomfort? What could you say to dispute that self-talk?
   • Identify two kinds of appropriate touch that you could use more frequently in your relationships with specific people. See if you can gradually increase your use of touch with them.

5. Assess the congruency between your verbal and nonverbal messages.
   • How do you feel when someone expresses a nonverbal message that is incongruent with his or her verbal message (for example, smiling while relating something painful or

PERSONAL ASSERTIVENESS INVENTORY

Relationship-enhancement Skills	Friends of the same sex	Friends of the opposite sex	Spouse, boyfriend/ girlfriend	Parents and in-laws	Children	Authority figures, Bosses, etc.	Business contacts, salespeople	Strangers
Can initiate conversations as desired								
Can maintain conversations								
Can end conversations as desired								
Can give compliments								
Can receive compliments without discounting them								
Can express love and affection comfortably								
Can deepen relationships when desired								

Self-protective Skills							
Can state my own feelings, beliefs, wishes attitudes or rights							
Can disagree with someone else's point of view comfortably							
Can comfortably refuse requests which conflict with my priorities							
Can defend self against unfair or inaccurate accusations							
Can express anger and annoyance assertively							
Can deal with someone else's anger comfortably and non-defensively							
Can make reasonable requests of others							

frustrating)? Why do you think people sometimes do this?

• Are you aware of situations where your nonverbal messages are incongruent with your verbal messages? What do you think you say to yourself subconsciously that causes you to give differing messages?

• What could you say to yourself to make yourself become comfortable in giving messages that are congruent verbally and nonverbally?

6. Take the two situations you identified in chapter 2 where you would like to become more assertive. Imagine yourself making those assertive statements accompanied by assertive nonverbal behavior. Visualize how you would be different, and what difference the assertive nonverbal behavior would make in how you feel as you are assertive.

7. Complete the Personal Assertive Inventory (following page), comparing your present responses with your responses at the beginning of the book. Use the following abbreviations: MI for much improved; I for improved; DNI for didn't need improvement and NI for not improved.

• Compare the number of areas where you have much improved, improved or didn't need improvement (MI, I, and DNI) with the number of areas where you haven't improved (NI). Are you satisfied with the number of areas in which you've made progress (or didn't need to change) in comparison with the areas where you haven't seen much progress?

• Identify three areas where you're most satisfied with your improvement.

• What factors have made it possible for you to change in those areas? (Possible factors can include, but are not limited to: understanding how you acquired a particular behavior, being able to dispute the mistaken belief that underlies a nonassertive response style, knowing what an alternative response would be, feeling support from others for change, having a safe place to practice changes before implementing them in "real life").

8. In what areas do you still want to improve? What can you do in the next month to enhance these skills?

AFTERWORD

The key concepts in Christian assertiveness are:

1. Assertiveness is a healthier and more biblical response to frustration than passivity, aggressiveness, passive-aggressiveness, or manipulation.

2. Assertiveness—an "I count me, I count you" approach to relationships—is consistent with the teaching that we are all created in the image of God and therefore have value and worth (Genesis 1:27; 9:6; James 3:9).

3. Assertiveness is foundational to Christian parenting. Relationship-enhancement skills—the abilities to motivate through encouragement, and to develop and deepen a friendship with a child—are basic to a child's development of a sense that he or she is valuable and lovable. Self-protective skills are necessary if a parent is to employ the loving discipline and spiritual leadership that will bring a child up in the nurture and admonition of the Lord.

4. Assertiveness is necessary if Christians are to give their brothers and sisters in Christ personal feedback that will help them grow in their awareness of how they impact others.

5. Assertiveness is necessary so that we do not allow the inevitable misunderstandings and conflicts that develop within the church body to grow into long-term resentments.

6. Assertiveness in a marriage relationship provides an important model for children of how to treat their future spouses with respect, and gives living instruction on how to maintain their own identities.

7. Assertiveness is the obvious choice, when compared with alternative ways of influencing people.

8. Assertiveness is modeled for us in the life of Christ and through what the Bible tells us about God the Father.

DIFFERENCES BETWEEN SECULAR AND CHRISTIAN ASSERTIVENESS

Secular	Christian
My highest goal is my own self-actualization. While respecting the rights of others, I will exercise my rights as fully as possible to achieve self-actualization.	My highest goals are to glorify God, to be an effective witness to the unsaved, and to be an agent of healing within Christ's body. I will on occasion suspend the exercise of my own rights in order to achieve one of these goals.
I exercise my rights in ways that do not violate yours, though I am still looking out for Number One.	My primary goal is to love and obey God. My secondary goal is to love and serve others. I find my deepest fulfillment through love and service to God and others.
I demand that you honor my rights!	I will do my best to honor your rights. I ask that you do the same to mine.

LIMITATIONS AND POTENTIAL DANGERS OF ASSERTIVENESS

We need to be aware of the limitations and potential dangers of assertiveness. First, without careful planning and prayer, assertiveness can become aggressiveness. God's wisdom is manifest in us when we are pure, peace-loving, considerate, submissive, and full of mercy (James 3:17). Christian assertiveness should always reflect these characteristics.

Second, without the use of regular affirmation in an assertive lifestyle, a person's assertive attempts may be perceived as aggressive, a perception we as Christians want to avoid.

Third, when assertive skills are wrongly used, they can promote a more selfish, self-centered, or manipulative lifestyle, rather than promoting a God-centered lifestyle.

Fourth, assertiveness is not a guarantee that we will always get what we want, even if we do everything in a healthy, assertive manner. The values of using Christian assertiveness are that we know how to build positive relationsips, we're less likely to damage relationships when differences arise, and we feel healthier because we're dealing with others from an "I count you, I count me" perspective.

Finally, the ability to be assertive doesn't mean we have to assert ourselves in every situation. In some cases it may be wiser to choose nonassertion or positive yielding. But we can be more confident knowing that *we do have a choice;* when we choose passivity, we're doing so because we decided that there is some higher goal for which we are striving.

GUIDELINES FOR GROUP LEADERS

Assertiveness as Two Kinds of Skills

Many people think of assertiveness primarily in terms of self-protective skills. The goal of this book and its exercises is to give significant emphasis to relationship-enhancement skills as well as to self-protective skills. There is a growing recognition that unless assertiveness is coupled with relationship affirmation, it can be destructive to relationships.

Since the goal of assertiveness is to help people become healthier as individuals and have healthier relationships, it is important that assertiveness training also helps people modify unhealthy relationships. Relationship-enhancement skills need to be developed before self-protective skills are practiced. People who want to move immediately to the self-protective skills without learning relationship-enhancement skills are at risk: assertiveness without affirmation is often viewed as aggressiveness by the recipient.[1]

The Theoretical Basis for This Model of Assertiveness Training

This book's approach to assertiveness training is based on behavioral psychology, cognitive psychology, and modeling principles from the work of Albert Bandura. Here are the ways that it draws on each of these approaches.

1. Behavioral psychology teaches that the most efficient way to help people develop healthy behavior is to identify their excessive or deficient behaviors and then help them change those behaviors. There is much emphasis in this book on teaching people new skills and helping them replace ineffective or unhealthy behaviors with effective and healthy ones.

2. Many people who live a nonassertive lifestyle do so because they are convinced, either consciously or subconsciously, that this is the most effective interpersonal stance for them to take. Unless they are persuaded that their style of behavior is faulty or ineffective or that they can choose better ways of responding, they will not be motivated to change. Therefore teaching them new behavioral skills must include addressing the mistaken beliefs that underlie their interpersonal style.[2] For this reason this book emphasizes elements from cognitive psychology, that is, helping the person identify faulty conscious or subconscious beliefs and replacing them with beliefs that support and justify an assertive lifestyle.

3. The third foundational source for the approach used in this book is Albert Bandura, who has demonstrated the importance of modeling as a rapid means of helping people acquire complex interpersonal skills (such as assertiveness).[3] His premise is that people who are *shown* how to do something will learn that skill more quickly than people who have to learn that skill through the process of trial and error. Therefore the exercises in this book, if used in a group setting, are designed to help people learn through modeling in two ways: either through the leader modeling the skill to be learned or through other group participants doing the same (vicarious learning).

Modeling is also used in another important way in this course (or group) experience. Many people are reluctant to change a long-established habit pattern: they have used it so long it has become part of their identity. Helping people see not only that many of their habits may have been developed as a result of human (usually parental) models but also that they may even have wished that those models had behaved differently seems to give them the freedom to relinquish their long-held habit more easily.

This book and its group exercises are designed with the belief that people will most easily be able to change complex interpersonal behaviors if they:
● Understand how they acquired a particular behavior,
● Dispute the mistaken belief that underlies that behavior

and replace that belief with one that would justify and support moving to a new behavior,

• Know what an alternative response would look and sound like,

• Feel support from others to try out the new behavior,

• Have a safe place to practice the new behavior before implementing it in "real life," and

• Receive coaching suggestions and positive feedback as they practice the new behavior in a safe setting.

Length of Group

This can be used as a ten- or twelve-week discussion class. A ten-week class would ordinarily spend one week on each chapter. A twelve-week class could spend two weeks on chapters 3 and 8, and one week on each of the others. By using the questions at the end of each chapter, the group could spend between forty-five and ninety minutes per session, depending on how many of the exercises are used.

Group Atmosphere

Try to build a positive, supportive group atmosphere that alleviates anxiety and encourages people to experiment with new ways of thinking and relating.

• First, be an encourager and look for what a person is doing right.

• Second, when making suggestions for change, focus on what the person did well before suggesting change.

• Third, give criticism in the form of positive suggestions rather than what the person did wrong (e.g., "Try to look at the person while you talk to her," rather than "You looked at your feet all the time you were talking.")

• Fourth, try not to give more than one (or at the most two) suggestions for the person to work on at a time. Most people aren't able to accept too much criticism at once or focus on changing more than one or two things at a time. If there are several behaviors the person needs to change, pick out one or two and mention them, then talk about others after the first behaviors have shown improvement.

● Fifth, don't allow the group members to begin analyzing each other: It's one thing to try to identify one's own cognitions, but quite another when group members try to psychoanalyze each other. The former is healthy, the latter is not. When people give feedback to others, they should focus on the other person's external behavior, not on the other person's internal thought processes.

● Sixth, keep the sessions positive by taking some time at the beginning of each one to allow people to share positive experiences in which they have tried to be assertive during the week. Such sharing can provide important modeling and encouragement for other group members as well as validation for those who were willing to try out their new skills.

Leading Class Discussion

Try to get the class themselves to answer as many of the questions that come up as possible. Knowledge that people discover for themselves, even if it takes considerable thinking on their part, makes more of an impact and is more likely to be used than information that is delivered by someone else. In some cases, if you believe a question is a very important one for people to answer for themselves and they can't do so within the class session, you can assign the question as homework for the next week.

Group Size

When leading this group for the first time, I would recommend six to twelve participants. After leading one or two groups, you can adjust group size depending on the needs of the situation and the size you can comfortably handle.

Confidentiality

During the first session (or a prescreening interview), stress that in order for each person to bring in real-life issues that he or she wants to work on, it is important that everything that is shared by someone else in the group be kept confidential. People may share what they've learned *about themselves* outside the group, but may not share anybody else's experience. You should ask each person to make this commitment to confidentiality before proceeding in the group, and should remind them once or twice more during the early weeks, so that this concept is firmly implanted in each member's mind. One breach of confidentiality can seriously impede other members' comfort in sharing real life issues.

Practical Needs

You will need a room large enough so that your group can break down into triads or quadrads during the discussion and role-play sessions and have a little distance between each small group. However, it's best that the room not be too large, since a huge room detracts from building the group's sense of cohesiveness. The room should preferably be carpeted to increase feelings of privacy and confidentiality.

The room needs a blackboard, a whiteboard, or newsprint and easel, so that you will have some means of writing down ideas during group discussions. For small groups you may wish to use newsprint and one of the two-foot by three-foot fiberboard easels that are available in some office supply stores. It is preferable that the room have chairs with writing arms on them so that people can more easily take notes.

Supply one copy of the Personal Assertiveness Inventory to each participant on weeks 1 and 9, and three copies of the nonverbal assertiveness checklist (exercise 1 in chapter 10) to each group member on week 9. It will probably be easier for you to make these copies en masse and distribute them than to have each person make their own.

Prior to the first session each person should purchase a copy of the book and read the introduction, first chapter, and do exercises 1 and 2 at the end of chapter 1. Individuals should also purchase their own six-by-nine-inch notebook to write their answers to exercises and keep notes on the group minilectures and discussions.

A more extensive Leader's Guide, designed for twelve forty-five minute or twelve ninety-minute groups, is available from the author for $15.00. This includes postage and handling. Victor Books can furnish you with his current address.

NOTES

Chapter 1

1. All names and real-life stories throughout this book have been modified to protect confidentiality.

2. Sherod Miller, Elam W. Nunnally, and Daniel B. Wackman, *Talking Together* (Minneapolis: Interpersonal Communications Programs, Inc., 1979), pp. 143–169.

3. *Ibid.*

4. *Ibid.*

5. *Ibid.*

Chapter 2

1. Albert Ellis, *Reason and Emotion in Psychotherapy.* (New York: Lyle Stewart, 1962).

2. M.M. Linehan, M.R. Goldfried and A.P. Goldfried. "Assertion Therapy: Skill Training or Cognitive Restructuring." *Behavior Therapy,* 1979, 10, pp. 372–388.

3. Albert Ellis, *Reason and Emotion in Psychotherapy,* (New York: Lyle Stewart, 1962).

4. After developing the Personal Assertiveness Inventory, I became aware of a very similar inventory developed by Charles Cerling. The two inventories were developed independently of each other.

Chapter 3

1. Paul Little, *How to Give Away Your Faith* (Downers Grove, Illinois: InterVarsity Press, 1966), p. 45.

2. Henry C. Lindgren, *An Introduction to Social Psychology* (New York: Wiley, 1969), pp. 23–51.

3. G.H. Mead, *Mind, Self and Society* (Chicago: University of Chicago Press, 1934).

4. Virginia Satir, Statement made in her training seminars in Atlanta and elsewhere.

5. John Powell, *Why Am I Afraid To Tell You Who I Am?* (Niles, Illinois: Argus Communications, 1969).

6. Dale Carnegie, *How To Win Friends and Influence People* (New York: Pocket Books, 1940), p. 62.

Chapter 4

1. William M. Counts, "The Nature of Man and the Christian's Self-Esteem." *Journal of Psychology and Theology,* Vol. 1, Issue 1, (January, 1973): 38–44.

2. Howard and Charlotte Clinebell, *The Intimate Marriage* (New York: Harper and Row, 1970) pp. 28–32.

3. Michael Campion, *Especially for Husbands* (Minneapolis: Bethany Fellowship, 1979).

4. Michael Campion, *Especially for Wives* (Minneapolis: Bethany Fellowship, 1979).

Chapter 5

1. John Stott, *Christian Counterculture,* (Downers Grove, Illinois: InterVarsity Press, 1978), pp. 57–68.

2. D. Carter and E. Rawlings (Eds.), *Psychotherapy for Women* (Springfield, Illinois: Charles C. Thomas, 1974).

3. Manuel J. Smith, *When I Say No, I Feel Guilty,* (New York: Bantam, 1975), pp. xv–xvi.

Chapter 6

1. I would like to acknowledge my indebtedness to Sherod Miller, Elam Nunnally, Daniel Wackman, and Phyllis Miller for the development of the Awareness Wheel as found in their book *Connecting* (Littleton, Colorado: Interpersonal Communication Programs, Inc., 1988), on which my discussion of the dimensions of self-awareness is based. At their request I am referring to the dimensions of self-awareness without using the Awareness Wheel graphic.

2. *Ibid.* p. 31.

Chapter 7

1. The Triple-A Model of Assertiveness is a modification of an earlier model of assertiveness known as the Kelly-Winship model, named after its creators Drs. George Kelley and Barbara Winship. Their model's components were Empathy, Assertion, and Action. Dr. George Kelley was a professor, and Barbara Winship a doctoral student at Georgia State University, and the model became known

in the Atlanta area through handouts and seminars. I have replaced the Empathy statement with an Affirmation statement because the Empathy statement often encouraged the assertor to "speak for the other" rather than "speaking for self," and because of the evidence indicating the importance of including Affirmation in assertive statements, evidence which will be discussed in the remainder of this chapter.

2. Discussion of procedure setting adapted from Sherod Miller, Elam Nunnally, and Daniel Wackman, *Talking Together,* (Minneapolis: Interpersonal Communications Programs, Inc., 1979), pp. 85–87.

3. D.B. Hull and H.E. Schroeder, "Some Interpersonal Effects of Assertion, Nonassertion and Aggression," *Behavior Therapy,* 10, (1979): pp. 20–28.

4. R.L. Woolfolk and S. Dever, "Perceptions of Assertion: An Empirical Analysis," *Behavior Therapy,* 10, (1979): pp. 404–411.

5. John Paul and David Augsburger, *Beyond Assertiveness,* (Waco, Texas: Word, 1980), p. 158.

Chapter 8

1. The concept of *detours* was first developed by Sharon and Gordon Bower in their book *Asserting Yourself,* (Reading, Massachusetts: Addison–Wesley, 1976), pp. 143–170.

2. *Ibid.*

3. Most assertive techniques have been so widely discussed in books, articles and workshops that it is hard to know who the original creator was. Sometimes techniques that are quite similar are given different names by different authors. The techniques discussed in this chapter are mentioned by one or more of the following authors:

(a) Robert Alberti and Michael Emmons, *Your Perfect Right* (San Luis Obispo, California: Impact, 1970).

(b) Manuel J. Smith, *When I Say No, I Feel Guilty* (New York: Bantam, 1975).

(c) Arthur J. Lange and Patricia Jakubowski, *Responsible Assertive Behavior* (Champaign, Illinois: Research Press, 1976).

(d) Sherwin Cotler and Julio Guerra, *Assertion Training* (Champaign, Illinois: Research Press, 1976).

(e) Sharon Bower and Gordon Bower, *Asserting Yourself* (Reading, Massachusetts: Addison–Wesley, 1976).

Chapter 9

1. Several of the workable compromises listed in this chapter are adapted from ideas in Virginia Satir, *Conjoint Family Therapy*, (Palo Alto: Science and Behavior Books, 1967), p. 14.

Chapter 10

1. For example, M. Hersen, R.M. Eisler, and P.M. Miller, "Development of Assertive Responses: Clinical, Measurement, and Research Considerations," *Behavior Research and Therapy*, 1973, Vol. 11, pp. 505–521. Joseph Wolpe and Arnold Lazarus, *Behavior Therapy Techniques*, (New York: Pergamon Press), 1966.

2. John T. Molloy, *Dress for Success*, (New York: Warner, 1975), p. 18.

3. John R. Hornbrook, *The Miracle of Touching* (Lafayette, Louisiana: Huntington House, 1985).

4. See footnotes 3 and 4 in chapter 7.

Group Leader Guidelines

1. D.B. Hull and H.E. Schroeder, "Some Interpersonal Effects of Assertion, Nonassertion and Aggression," *Behavior Therapy*, 10, (1979): 20–28. Robert L. Woolfolk and Sharon Dever, "Perceptions of Assertion: An Empirical Analysis," *Behavior Therapy*, 10, (1979): pp. 404–411.

2. See Patricia Jakubowski-Spector, "Facilitating the Growth of Women through Assertive Training," *The Counseling Psychologist*, 4, (1973): 75–86 and Marsha Linehan, Marvin Goldfried, and Anita Goldfried, "Assertion Therapy: Skill Training or Cognitive Restructuring?" *Behavior Therapy,*10, (1979): pp. 372–388.

3. Albert Bandura, "Psychotheraphy Based on Modeling Principles," *Handbook of Psychotherapy and Behavior Change*. Edited by A. Bergin and S. Garfield (New York: Wiley, 1971), pp. 653–708.